GASTRIC SLEEVE BARIATRIC

Gastric Sleeve Bariatric Cookbook - 250 Healthy Recipes For Take Care Of Your New Stomach, Learn How to Keep The Weight Loss Post Operation, Fight The Food Addiction With A Delicious Meal Plan.

Tasha Pope

© Copyright 2021 by Tasha Pope - All rights reserved.

This document is geared towards providing exact and reliable information in regard to the topic and issue covered.

- From a Declaration of Principles which was accepted and approved equally by a Committee of the American Bar Association and a Committee of Publishers and Associations.

In no way is it legal to reproduce, duplicate, or transmit any part of this document in either electronic means or in printed format. All rights reserved.

The information provided herein is stated to be truthful and consistent, in that any liability, in terms of inattention or otherwise, by any usage or abuse of any policies, processes, or directions contained within is the solitary and utter responsibility of the recipient reader. Under no circumstances will any legal responsibility or blame be held against the publisher for any reparation, damages, or monetary loss due to the information herein, either directly or indirectly.

Respective authors own all copyrights not held by the publisher.

The information herein is offered for informational purposes solely and is universal as so. The presentation of the information is without contract or any type of guarantee assurance.

The trademarks that are used are without any consent, and the publication of the trademark is without permission or backing by the trademark owner. All trademarks and brands within this book are for clarifying purposes only and are owned by the owners themselves, not affiliated with this document.

Table of Contents

- Your New Bariatric Lifestyle & Your New Mindset Changing Your Habits & Creating Lifestyle Change 14
- Tips for After Surgery 19
- Meal Plan Challenge 21
- Soups 25
  - Bean Tomato Broth 25
  - Collard Greens Soup Topped With Sage Mushrooms 25
  - Carrot and Potato Soup 26
  - Red Pepper and Tomato Soup 27
  - Slow Cooker Chicken Soup With Baby Spinach Leaves 27
  - Thai Chicken Soup 27
  - Cumin and Turmeric Fish Stew 28
  - Cabbage Soup With Arugula Leaves 29
  - Turkey Goulash With Baby Spinach Leaves 29
  - Carrot and Turkey Soup 29
  - Fennel and Ginger Chicken Soup With Asparagus Tips 30
  - Spinach Veal Broth 31
  - Celery Spinach Broth 31
  - Carrot Coconut Broth 32
  - Eggplant Tomato Soup 32
  - Acorn Squash Cream Soup 33
  - Creamy Leek Soup 33
  - Green Cream Soup 34
  - Spinach Potato Cream Soup 34
  - Chicken Cauliflower Soup 35
  - Zucchini Cream Soup 35

- Broccoli Gorgonzola Soup 35
- Chickpea Pepper Soup 36
- Fresh Tomato and Celery Soup 36

Creamy Wild Asparagus Soup 37
- Homemade Chicken Soup 37
- Butternut Squash Soup 37
- Simple Meatball Soup 38
- Chicken Barley Soup 38
- Ham and Bean Soup 39
- French Onion Soup 39
- Cheesy Cauliflower Soup 39
- Creamy Chicken Vegetable Soup 40
- Clam Chowder 40
- Cream of Broccoli Soup 41
- Chicken Noodle Soup 41
- Cream of Potato Soup 41
- Chicken and Bean Soup 42
- Chicken Ramen Soup Broth 42
- Carrot, Ginger Gusto Apple Soup 43
- Carrot, Ginger Zest Chicken Orangey Soup 20 43
- Lemony Chicken Soup Broth 44

Super Soup 44
- Tomato bisque 45
- Smoky soup V 45
- Onion and Peas Soup 45
- Curried Carrot, Sweet Potato, and Ginger Soup V 46

- .... **Breakfast**
.... 47
- Lettuce power pack 47

- Greek egg muffins 47
- Sunday morning special 47

Lemony Raspberries Bowls 47

Pancetta and Spinach Frittata 48

Chicken and Zucchini Omelet 49

Breakfast Pea Tortilla 49

Mushroom Cheese Salad 49

Blueberry Chia Overnight Oats 50

Carrot Oatmeal 50

Pumpkin Pie Bliss Protein Shake 51

Apricot Overnight Oatmeal Recipe 51

Souffle Omelet With Mushrooms 51

- Simple sunshine scramble 52
- Black beans puree with scrambled eggs 53
- Veggie quiche muffins 53
- Steel cut oat blueberry pancakes 53
- Very berry muesli 54
- Strawberry & mushroom breakfast sandwich 54
- Shakshuka egg bake 54
- Ricotta baked in the oven 55
- Poached eggs Italian style 55
- Denver egg muffins with ham crust 55
- Cheesy slow cooker egg casserole 55
- Make-ahead breakfast burritos 56
- Baked broccoli and eggs 57
- Black bean and pumpkin soup 57
- Broccoli and tofu quiche 57
- Cheese-filled acorn squash 58
- Cheesy spinach bake 59

- Southwestern Scrambled Egg Burritos 59
- Smoothie Bowl With Greek Yogurt And Fresh Berries 59

Cherry-Vanilla Baked Oatmeal 60

High-Protein Pancakes 61

Pumpkin Muffins With Walnuts And Zucchini 61

- Hard-Boiled Eggs And Avocado On Toast 61
- Yogurt- Based Breakfast Popsicles 62
- Shrimp Ceviche 62
- Chicken Caprese 63
- Black Bean and Corn Salad 63

Soft Eggs with Chives and Ricotta 64

- Mocha Frappuccino 64
- Oatmeal Cookie Shake 64
- Bun less Breakfast Sandwich 65

Ham and Egg Roll-Ups 65

Chocolate Porridge 65

- Flour-Less Pancakes 65
- Cheesy Spiced Pancakes 66
- Egg Muffin 66
- Cottage Cheese Pancakes 67
- Sheet Pan Zucchini Parmesan 68
- Grilled Fig And Peach Arugula Salad With Ricotta Salute And A Black Pepper Vinagretteprint 68

Honey Mustard Pork Tenderloin 69

Chicken Simmered With Black Beans 69

Greek Baked Chicken 69

Sweet and Tangy Chicken With Pumpkin Purée 70

Country Style Pork Tenderloin 71

Simple Beef Sirloin Roast 71

Shrimp, Zucchini and Cherry Tomato Sauce 72

Baked Parmesan and Herb Coated Chicken Strips 72

Low-Carb Chicken Tortillas 73

Stuffed Chicken 73

Lean Spring Stew 73

- Yummy Chicken Bites 74
- Shrimp Scampi 74
- Zucchini Frittata 75
- Salmon Patties 75
- Apple Cinnamon Oatmeal 75
- Stuff Cheese Pork Chops 75
- Italian Pork Chops 76
- Sunshine Wrap 76
- Taco Omelet 77
- Sheet Pan Spicy Tofu And Green Beans 77
- Skillet Chicken Thighs With Potato, Apple, And Spinach 77

Apple Cider Glazed Chicken Breast With Carrots 79

- Onion Paprika Pork Tenderloin 79
- Rosemary Garlic Pork Chops 79
- Skinny Chicken Pesto Bake 80
- Cold Tomato Couscous 80
- Fresh Shrimp Spring Rolls 80
- Chicken Breast Tortilla 81
- Sweet Roasted Beet & Arugula Tortilla Pizza V 81
- Southwestern Black Bean Cakes with Guacamole 81

Veggie Quesadillas with Cilantro Yogurt Dip 81

- Mayo-less Tuna Salad 82

Southwest Style Zucchini Rice Bowl 82

- Pesto & Mozzarella Stuffed Portobello Mushroom Caps 82
- Tandoori Chicken 83

- Turkey Fajitas Bowls 83
- Baked Chicken Pesto 83

Spaghetti Squash Lasagna V 83

Crab Mushrooms 84

- Loaded Sweet Potatoes 84
- Coconut Flour Spinach Casserole 85
- Tilapia With Cherry Tomatoes 85
- Strawberry Frozen Yogurt Squares 85
- Smoked Tofu Quesadillas 85
- Zucchini Pizza Boats 86
- Pear-Cranberry Pie with Oatmeal Streusel 86
- Mixed Sweet Potatoes 87

Asparagus and Parmesan 87

Walnut and Cheese Filled Mushrooms 87

Chard With Cheddar 88

Herbed Tomatoes 88

Cream Potato 89

Grilled Tomatoes With Black Garlic Spread 89

Tomato and Arugula Egg White Scramble 89

Sunshine Pie 90

Low-Fat Fish Tacos With Kale Leaves 91

Wild Salmon Salad 91

- Air Fried Spinach Casserole 91
- Fresh Shrimp Spring Rolls V 20 92

Southwestern Black Bean Cakes with Guacamole V 93

- Veggie Quesadillas with Cilantro Yogurt Dip V 93
- Mayo-less Tuna Salad 20 93
- Southwest Style Zucchini Rice Bowl 20 94

Pesto & Mozzarella Stuffed Portobello Mushroom Caps V 94

- Pear, Turkey and Cheese Mushroom Sandwich 20 94
- Salmon Salad Pita 20 95
- Thai Tofu Quinoa Bowl 95
- One-Skillet Peanut Chicken 95
- Turkey Stuffed Zucchini Boats – Italian Style 96
- Tomato Baked Tilapia with Lemon 97
- Stuffed Poblano Peppers 20 97
- Whole Wheat BLT 97
- Massaman Curry Chicken with Sweet Potatoes & Peas 98
- Coconut Adobo Chicken Stuffed Sweet Potatoes 98
- Fennel Quiche V 99
- Southwest Tortilla Bake V 99
- Cucumber Tuna Salad 99
- Roasted Parmesan Cauliflower 100
- Delicious Chicken Salad 100
- Cauliflower Broth 101
- Cauliflower Mash 101
- Curried Egg Salad 101
- Dijon Potato Salad 102
- Carrot Sweet Potato Soup 102
- Creamy Salmon Salad 103
- Baked Dijon Salmon 103
- Dijon Chicken Thighs 103
- Herb Pork Chops 103
- Taco Chicken 104
- Broiled Fish Fillet 104
- Chicken Skewers 105
- Grilled Chicken Breasts 105
- Chili Garlic Salmon 105

- •Baked Lemon Tilapia 106

Dessert and Snacks 107

- • Garlic Bread 107
- Chocolate Soufflé 107
- Cream Cheese Wontons 107
- Angel Food Cake 108
- Chocolate Brownies With Almond Butter 108
- Lemon Blackberry Frozen Yogurt 109
- Low-Calorie Cherry Chocolate Ice Cream 109
- Skinny Mug Brownie 109
- Carrot Cake 109
- Mini Plum Cakes 110
- Lemonade Cupcakes 111
  - • Mozzarella Bites 111
  - • Ranch Pretzels 111
  - • Maple Barbecue Cashews 111
  - • Pizza Bread 111
  - • Mexican Corn 112
  - • Smoky Chickpeas 112
  - • Potato Chips 112
  - • Roasted Macadamia 112
  - • Apricot Brie Snack 113
  - • Garlic-Parmesan Cheesy Chips 113
  - • Cheesy Baked Radish Chips 113
  - • Savory Cheese Biscuits 113
  - • Italian Herb Muffins 114
  - • Cheesy Cauliflower Tots 114
  - • Mozzarella Mushroom Caps 114
  - • Almond-Crusted Mozzarella Sticks 115

- Almond Light-as-Air Cookies 115
- Strawberry Gelatin Tea 115
- Subtly Sweet Coconut Milk "Flan" 116
- Chia Chocolate Pudding 116

Simply Vanilla Frozen Greek Yogurt 116
- Mashed Cauliflower 117
- Baked Zucchini Fries 117
- Pickle Roll-Ups 117
- Tomato, Basil, And Cucumber Salad 118
- Raspberry Sorbet 118
- Avocado Hummus 118
- Avocado Detox Smoothie 119
- Sweet Pumpkin Pudding 119
- Beet Spinach Salad 119
- Grilled Avocado in Curry Sauce 120

Broccoli Cauliflower Puree 120
- Peanut butter joy cookies 120
- Chocolate almond ginger mousse 121

Bella's apple crisp 121

Red energy wonders 121
- Chocolate protein pudding pops 122
- Strawberry frozen yogurt 122
- Lemon mousse 122
- Mozzarella Balls Recipe 123
- Chocolate Protein Balls 123
- Instant Frozen Berry Yogurt 123
- Chocolate Avocado Pudding 123
- Mixed Berry Popsicles 124

- .... Conclusion
.... 125

- Introduction

In recent years, the gastric sleeve has been one of the most used procedures for weight loss.

The "gastric sleeve" refers to a simple operation in which part of the stomach is removed and turned into a tube that limits food intake.

That said, in spite of its efficacy in terms of weight loss, not everyone who needs such an intervention can access it due to its high cost.

However, thanks to new advances in medicine which include robotic surgery and 3D printing, we hope this procedure will soon be more accessible to all those who need it.

Gastric sleeve is a method of reducing the size of the stomach that removes part of it. To achieve a hundred percent weight loss, other methods must be used as well.

The gastric sleeve has many benefits: it has the capacity to reduce the amount of food consumed by up to 30% as compared to before, it is easy to maintain and results can be seen right away.

In addition, one month after surgery patients should have returned to eating normal amounts of food without gaining weight or experiencing any side effects.

For these reasons, gastric sleeve has become an extremely popular procedure for both men and women who wish to lose weight.

Among the people who choose to undergo surgery to achieve weight loss are both those who suffer from health problems associated with obesity and those who only wish to look better in their clothes.

The gastric sleeve is mainly used as a method of losing weight, but it is also used by those undergoing bariatric surgery.

This type of surgery focuses on patients who are at risk of developing serious illnesses due to their obesity, and thus must lose weight to prevent such illnesses from manifesting.

A good example would be diabetes: this illness occurs due to diet and lifestyle factors that lead to insulin resistance, which eventually causes diabetes.

A gastric sleeve could be used to prevent or treat diabetes.

In fact, many patients who already have diabetes have seen great results using a gastric sleeve to overcome this disease.

Besides a reduction in weight, there are other advantages to bariatric surgery such as a decrease in appetite, which leads to greater self-control and greater metabolic rate.

Since this type of surgery requires hospitalization, it is expensive and therefore not everyone can afford it. In fact, many people cannot even access the procedure because many health plans do not offer them coverage for such surgeries.

The cost of bariatric surgery is one of the major barriers preventing people from getting the help they need.

This is why so many people have turned to gastric sleeve as an alternative.

By opting for this method, patients can get the benefits of bariatric surgery without the need for a traditional hospitalization.

The next step in its development would be 3D printed surgery, which would allow surgeons to eliminate the issues related to traditional surgery (such as infection or damage to internal organs) with minimal risk.

The gastric sleeve procedure was first developed in the 1940s and used during this time as a means for weight loss, but only as a temporary solution until other alternatives could be found.

It was introduced with wide attention after the release of the Atkins diet in 1972 by Dr. Robert Atkins.

Today, gastric sleeve is well known as a method of losing weight.

In fact, it is considered one of the simplest and most effective solutions for those who want to lose weight and even as an alternative to bariatric surgery.

It is used to treat not only overweight people but also those who are simply trying to get back in shape.

A person's body mass index (BMI) must be higher than 35 in order for him or her to qualify for this surgery. Patients with a BMI greater than 40 are generally considered obese, and those with a BMI greater than 45 should undergo gastric bypass surgery instead of a gastric sleeve.

In a gastric sleeve surgery, the stomach is reduced by turning part of it into a thin tube about 15 to 25 millimeters long.

The operation is minimally invasive and can be performed under local anesthesia.

It usually takes between 30 and 45 minutes to perform the procedure, which involves making a small incision in the abdomen and removing part of the stomach.

Once this has been done, another section of the stomach is connected to what remains.

The new gastric sleeve that forms acts as a restriction that limits food intake, thus helping patients lose weight.

The operation causes only temporary discomfort to patients, and most are able to leave hospital after 24 hours after surgery.

> - Your New Bariatric Lifestyle & Your New Mindset Changing Your Habits & Creating Lifestyle Change

- *Steps and Strategies for Success*

Before your surgery, there are some things you can do ahead of time that will help you during those painful days.

- *Change your diet.*

You need to preparation timer your body for this direction by going on a high-protein liquid diet one or two weeks before your surgery. This will shrink your liver, making the surgery safer for you.

- *Change your grocery list.*

You need to have a lot of protein-rich liquids before surgery and after surgery. Clear liquids are what you will consume immediately after your surgery for a day or two. After that phase, you will advance to protein shakes and pureed food.

- *Get the clothes you will need.*

You will need transition clothes for the various weights that you will be. You will want your initial clothing after the surgery to fit loosely. You will also want slip-on shoes so that you won't have to bend over to tie your shoes.

- *Stop smoking.*

Surgeons take smoking seriously. Just before surgery, they will likely give you a blood test to see whether you have been smoking lately. If you have, they will cancel your surgery. Why? If you are smoke-free, your recovery will be quicker. You will need to quit smoking one month before your surgery.

- *Pack your hospital bag.*

You will stay at the hospital one night, so pack whatever you will need for one night.

- *Preparation timer your support group.*

You will need both physical and mental support after your surgery. You need to educate people before your surgery and line volunteers up who can help you while you recover.

- *Get your insurance or other financing source ready.*

Heck if your insurance pays for this kind of surgery. Typically, body mass index and other health issues are involved. Get the financials ready to pay for your surgery.

- *Get ahead of the household chores and shopping before surgery.*

Make lots of smoothies (minus the ice cubes), cook and freeze meals, clean the house, and do all of the laundry before you go in for surgery so that nobody has to do those things later. Buy the stool softeners, over-the-counter medications and your prescriptions (if possible) ahead of time.

Your friends and family may help you, but it would be easier for everyone if you have most of the work done ahead of time. You will also be certain to not lack for anything while you are at a disadvantage.

- *Get the facts.*

Talk to your surgeon about any concerns or questions you have about your surgery so that you have a good understanding about what will be done and be less anxious about your surgery.

- *Study up on proteins.*

You will need to consume a lot of protein after your surgery. You need to try protein powders to discover which ones you like among the ones that won't add a lot of calories. Food sources are peanut butter, legumes, chicken, meats, and protein shakes.

After your surgery

- *Follow your doctor's prescribed diet.*

Eat what your doctor tells you to eat after your surgery, which will consist of a lot of liquid. If you eat regular food too early or if you eat sugary or fat food, you may damage your stomach or harm yourself.

- *Skip work until you have healed.*

Depending on which kind of surgery you have and what type of work you do, you could be back to work as soon as two weeks after surgery if you do not lift anything heavy.

- *Exercise when you can.*

Wait about four weeks before you exercise or lift weights so that you will decrease the chance that you will get a hernia in the wound.

- *Go to your check-ups.*

Let your doctor check on your progress at the scheduled times. He'll see whether or not you are on schedule in your weight loss goals.

- *Continue to find suitable foods you can eat.*

You need to try out new recipes so that you can stay on your diet plan. You don't want boredom with your food to turn you back to your old eating habits.

- *Take multivitamins.*

It will be hard to get all of the nutrition that you need from just your food, especially less food, so be sure to take a multivitamin daily.

- *Know when to ask for help.*

Right after your surgery, it will be hard to get anything done. Hopefully, you got your chores done, groceries and meds purchased, food pre-made and frozen, and your helpers lined up before you went into surgery. Don't be afraid to call on the friends and family who agreed to help you when you need them, especially if you notice a complication.

- *Follow your prescription.*

Keep taking your prescribed medication for as long as you were supposed to take it. Don't get off of it early. Make an appointment with your doctor if you have discomfort beyond what is normal.

- *Count the calories.*

If you keep your calorie intake between 600 and 800 per day, you will lose weight. Consult your doctor for his suggested calorie target. Don't eat high-calorie food, especially those with sugar and/or fat.

- *Don't drink your calories.*

Drink water, unsweetened ice tea, and sugar-free juice. You will need to use up your daily allotment of calories on food that contains protein instead of drinks with "empty calories."

- **Post Operation Life**

- *Post-op gastric bypass surgery diet*

The moment the surgery is completed, your new diet begins in full force. The aim of the diet is to help you recover in the best way possible. The gastric bypass diet comes in various stages. Each stage shows that you are healing a little bit more. As you progress, you can go a little higher in your gastric bypass surgery diet. For easy remembering, the gastric bypass surgery has been divided into 5 stages. These stages do not include the pre-op diet. They are simply for the post-op diet.

Stage 1- Clear liquids

The first stage includes only liquids. This stage starts after the surgery. For about 1-7 days after the surgery, the patient can take only clear liquids. Your dietician will let you know exactly how long to stay in this stage.

Stage 2A-Full liquid

This diet includes full liquids. Full liquids are semi-liquid and are not see-through. It is midway between clear liquids and pureed foods. Here, your liquids can start to have some chunks of solid foods. This stage lasts for 1-2 weeks

Stage 2B- Pureed foods

After that stage, this next one lasts for 1-2 weeks. Here, you can consume liquid forms of protein. You should be taking up to 70 grams of protein and 64 ounces of fluids.

Stage 3- Soft foods

In this stage, patients can begin to eat soft foods that can be easily mashed. You should be taking up to 70 grams of protein and 64 ounces of clear water. You should also eat about 1-2 ounces in each serving. You should also take a very little portion of healthy fats. Usually, this comes from an avocado.

Stage 4- Solid foods

Here you can go back to eating solid foods. This diet starts from that point to the rest of your life. You should eat mainly protein and vegetables. The grains you consume should be in limited quantities. Your intake of sugar should be at the barest minimum. This will be your stage for the rest of your life.

- *Dos and don'ts of gastric bypass surgery diet*

As expected, there are some things you are simply not allowed to do when it comes to your gastric bypass diet. Here are some of them.

1. No straw- This applies from stage 1 to stage 3. You should not use straws to take in your liquids. This is because using straws can take in unwanted air into the stomach.

2. Do not eat more than one new food per day- Your body will have different reactions to new foods even though you have eaten them before the surgery. Anything you haven't eaten after the surgery is a new food. Do not try more than one per day.

3. *Learn how to chew-* The way that you used to chew before the surgery is no longer the way you will chew. Before, chewing was a careless thing we did. However, now, you must learn how to chew again. Time yourself to ensure that you chew each bite for as long as 15-seconds.

4. *Drink water-* At stage four, drink at least 64 ounces of water each day. Take water 30 minutes after food.

5. *Avoid processed carbs and sugar-* Stay away from foods that have high levels of sugar and refined or processed carbohydrates

6. *Stay away from unhealthy fats-* Make sure you avoid foods that have unhealthy fat.

7. *Learn how to eat-* Learn to chew proteins first. When they are eaten, eat your vegetables, and then carbohydrates.

- *Food cravings after gastric surgery*

After your gastric bypass surgery you may find that you encounter a lot of cravings. It is only natural and you can be assured that after some time, your body will adjust and you will have few cravings. In case you have cravings, here are some tips to help you manage them.

1. *Invest in healthy snacks-* Purchase healthy snacks. When you purchase healthy snacks, you can have them when you are hungry to take your mind off food cravings.

2. *Do not skip meals-* To succeed in this diet, you must find balance. Finding your balance involves eating when you should and when you shouldn't. Skipping one meal can put in discord to your hard work as your stomach is now extremely sensitive.

3. *Drink water-* In a day, ensure you have as much as 8 glasses. When you are craving, take a big gulp or two.

4. *Plan your environments-* Do not go to a fast food restaurant where everyone will be eating what you can't eat. Plan your environments. Plan where you are supposed to stay.

5. *Distract yourself-* Distracting yourself when you are cravings will help you out. Get up and do something you like.

Tips for After Surgery

You'll also want to read up on some tips for handing things after the surgery as well. For example, your entire lifestyle ahead will be in for a lot of change. You won't be allowed to eat anything for several days to allow your stomach to heal up, and your diet in the recovery period will be drastically different. How often you make to the medical clinic will also increase so your health can be monitored and you can have your blood tested.

Your entire body and even your mental state (hopefully temporarily!) will be different than it was before. As you begin to lose weight at a rapid weight, you'll feel things such as body aches, fatigue, feeling cold, thinning hair, and dry skin. How you handle these changes in your life will be just as important as how you handle preparations for before the gastric sleeve surgery as well.

Here are some tips for after gastric sleeve surgery:

- *Listen to Your Doctor!*

You don't want to go through the entire surgical procedure only to not lose as much weight as you expected you would. Following the specific instructions set to you by your doctor will be the most important thing you can do to ensuring the aftermath of the gastric sleeve surgery is successful. Besides, don't avoid any check-ups with your doctor as well. While medical check-ups may be time-consuming, they are important to keeping you on the right track.

- *Only Work When You Are Ready*

If you feel physically uncomfortable about returning to work during the recovery time, that's perfectly fine. In fact, the average patient of gastric sleeve surgery takes up to two weeks before they are fully healed enough to head back to work. Don't feel ashamed if you don't feel you are ready yet.

- *Get Plenty of Exercises*

It will take time to get into the habit of exercise and to exercise successfully, but doing so will allow your body to strengthen and dealing with the loss of calorie intake. You can start some simple exercise programs, such as walking, swimming.

- *Learn More*

Don't hesitate to continue to learn as much more as you can after the surgery. You can look into what new recipes you can try or what some different exercising tips that exist out there.

- *Receive Plenty of Support*

Any patient who goes through gastric sleeve surgery will need the support of family and friends following the surgery. Don't feel nervous about asking for help. In fact, most of the people you are close with will probably be glad to help you along on your journey.

- *Take Your Medications*

Don't try to phase out of taking your medication. If you have any discomfort with your existing medication, speak with your doctor or a member of the medical staff before quitting taking them. If you don't follow your medical prescription, the surgery may not be as successful as it should be. In addition to your medications, take plenty of multivitamins. Multivitamins should be prescribed to you anyway, but if they aren't, know that multivitamins are necessary for your body to get the nutrition it loses from the decrease in food intake.

- *Calories*

Calories, calories, calories. Obviously, by consuming less food your body will be in taking fewer calories. However, you also want to keep yourself at 600 to 800 calories per day; otherwise, the aftermath of the surgery may not be a success. If the specific number of calories you need to intake is different than the typical six hundred to eight hundred range, your doctor will let you know. Keep track of your daily caloric intake and educate yourself on how much calories are in the foods and liquids you consume. If you can adhere to a daily regimen, you'll keep your calorie intake right where it needs to be.

- *Avoid Alcohol*

Finally, you'll want to avoid drinking alcohol after surgery. Doing so can have drastic effects on your recovery time and of your weight loss in general.

Meal Plan Challenge

Planning your meals

Have an idea of what you plan to eat throughout the week will save you lots of time and money, and it will also minimize the choices you need to make around meals. Now, I don't want you to be overwhelmed with the idea of meal planning. It doesn't have to be time-consuming or difficult, and your plan certainly does not need to be followed to a t. Start simple, and think of a few ideas of what you might like to have for breakfasts, lunches, dinners, and snacks in between. Make sure you have the ingredients you'll need on hand, and then you'll have options when it comes time to eat.

Meal-planning tips

Choose recipes with the same ingredients to reduce food waste and save money.

Choose a shopping day, and make a shopping list before you go. Keep breakfasts and snacks simple. Cook once; eat twice. Freeze leftovers for easy meals throughout the week.

The 10-week meal plan

Your surgeon's recommendations may differ from this transitional plan, so be sure to consult with your doctor before advancing between phases.

As part of the plan, you will find ideas for how to incorporate physical activity into your life. These exercises are tailored to each stage of your recovery.

Adaptations for band and sleeve patients

Gastric band, sleeve, and bypass directions vary widely in surgical complexity, which will dictate the length of recovery and transition back to regular textures in your diet. Always consult with your care team before making any dietary changes, but here are some guidelines for adjusting the meal plan to your specific needs.

Adjustable gastric band

Most gastric band patients will progress to soft foods after 4 weeks and a general diet after 5 or 6 weeks. However, roughly 6 weeks after your band placement, you may receive your first saline fill. After your band is placed, and following each subsequent fill, you will need to adhere to a transitional diet, from full liquids back to solids as tolerated, usually over a span of 7 to 10 days.

Laparoscopic sleeve gastrectomy

Due to the complexity of the gastric sleeve surgeries, the length of transitional diet and recovery periods are different from patient to patient. Typically, sleeve patients follow a full-liquid diet for 2 weeks, a purée diet for another week, and a soft-foods diet for 3 weeks before returning to normal textures as tolerated 6 weeks post-op.

The first 8 weeks

A transitional diet in the first 8 weeks after surgery is essential for proper healing. Be sure to stay mindful while you eat, as you may not have a true understanding of the capacity of your new pouch. If you have any difficulty after advancing your diet to the next phase, return to the previous stage for a few days.

- *Liquids*

After surgery, you'll begin with a full-liquid diet. Liquid textures require minimal work for your stomach to digest, allowing it to heal appropriately. Your primary goal during this stage is to stay hydrated, but you will also be using protein drinks to reach your protein targets necessary for recovery.

- *Puréed foods*

After 1 to 2 weeks tolerating liquids, you can begin transitioning to a purée diet. Foods at this stage should have the consistency of a smooth paste—no solid pieces or chunks. Foods that purée well include soft meats with sauce, fruits, cooked vegetables, low-fat dairy items, eggs, low-fiber hot cereals, legumes, and low-fat soups. Most can be puréed in a good blender or food processor.

Because of stomach capacity restrictions, you will want to limit your portions to about 2 to 3 ounces (4 to 8 tablespoons) at a time. Consider adding unflavored protein powder or fat-free powdered milk to your foods, or continue using protein shakes to reach your protein goal (at least 60 grams per day).

As you transition from liquids to purées, it is important you stay hydrated, drinking 48 ounces of fluids per day, including protein shakes. Also remember that you shouldn't drink with meals; wait at least 30 min after you finish eating.

Now that your body's healing, you can begin low-impact exercises to build strength and flexibility. You can also begin taking longer walks, or walking more quickly.

- *Helpful tips:*

If you experience changes in taste, like a sensitivity to sweetness, consider adding spices or dried herbs to food and shakes.

If you have nausea or discomfort while eating, take smaller bites, and make sure you eat very slowly.

If you do not have much of an appetite, continue using protein shakes to meet your daily goals.

If you are having difficulty tolerating meats, try something softer, with more moisture.

If you are having difficulty drinking enough fluids (48 to 64 ounces per day), use protein shakes to reach your protein goal and stay hydrated. If you are not feeling hungry, set alarms to remind yourself to eat.

Try only 1 or 2 new foods at a time.

- *Soft foods*

A soft-foods diet offers more texture for your tastes, but you still need to be able to cut through your food with a fork. Food pieces should be small, tender, and easy to chew. As you transition to a soft-foods diet, make sure you try only one or two new foods at a time. Some possibilities for this stage include ground lean meat or poultry, flaky fish, eggs, cottage cheese, yogurt, soft cheese, hot cereal, canned or soft fresh fruits (without seeds or skin), cooked vegetables (without skin), beans, and lentils.

You will likely be eating at least 3 meals with 1 to 2 protein-rich snacks or shakes to meet your goal of 60 to 80 grams of protein per day. Each meal should consist of 1/3 to ½ cup of food. Continue to avoid drinking while you eat. Wait 30 min after a meal to hydrate.

Soups

Bean Tomato Broth

Preparation time: 15 minutes
Cooking time: 1 hour 20 minutes
Servings: 6
Ingredients:
2 lbs medium-sized tomatoes, pureed
1 cup kidney beans, pre-cooked
1 small onion, diced
2 garlic cloves, crushed
1 cup heavy cream
1 cup vegetable broth
2 tbsp fresh parsley, finely chopped
¼ tsp black pepper, ground
2 tbsp extra-virgin olive oil
1 tsp dry oregano, ground
½ tsp salt
¼ tsp chili pepper, ground

Directions:
Soak the beans overnight. Rinse and drain well and place the beans in a deep pot. Add 4 cups of water and bring it to a boil. Cook for 30 minutes and then remove from the heat. Drain and set aside.

Wash the tomatoes and cut into bite-sized pieces. Transfer to a food processor and add some salt and oregano. Blend until smooth and creamy and set aside.

Now, preheat the oil in a large saucepan over medium-high temperature. Add onions and garlic and stir-fry for 5 minutes, or until translucent. Add beans, tomatoes, and broth. Stir well and bring it to a boil. Reduce the heat to low and sprinkle with chili. Stir well and cook for 35-40 minutes. Add heavy cream and cook for 2 more minutes, stirring constantly.

Remove from the heat and set aside to cool for a while. Now, drain the liquid into a serving bowl. Sprinkle with some finely chopped parsley and enjoy!

Nutrition: Calories: 254, Protein: 9.7g, Total Carbs: 27.1g, Dietary Fibers: 6.9g, Total Fat: 13g

Collard Greens Soup Topped With Sage Mushrooms

Preparation time: 10 minutes
Cooking time: 50 minutes
Servings: 3
Ingredients

- 1 tsp. olive oil
- 1 tsp. smoked paprika
- 1 tsp. cumin
- 2 medium carrots, sliced
- 2 C. water
- ½ C. cherry tomatoes
- 3 tbsps. lemon juice
- A pinch of freshly ground black pepper to taste
- 2 C. collard greens, loosely packed, big stems removed

For the sage mushrooms:

- 1 tsp. olive oil cooking spray
- ½ C. of shiitake mushrooms
- 1 tsp. dried sage

Directions

1. Heat the olive oil in a nonstick soup pot over low heat and gently fry the paprika and cumin.
2. Increase to medium heat and add the carrots and ¼ C. of water.
3. Cover and cook for 10 minutes, stirring occasionally.
4. Add in the rest of the soup's ingredients and increase to medium-high heat to let the soup come to a boil.
5. Reduce the heat to medium, and let the soup simmer uncovered for 30–35 minutes, or until the vegetables are tender. While the soup is simmering, sauté the shiitake mushrooms.

To make the shiitake mushrooms:

1. Lightly spray a nonstick frying pan with olive oil cooking spray.
2. Allow the pan to get very hot before adding the mushrooms as this will prevent the mushrooms from releasing their liquids when the mushrooms are wilted, season with the dried sage.
3. Serve the soup with a sprinkling of sage mushrooms.

Nutrition
- Calories: 101 kcal.
- Protein: 3 g.
- Total carbs: 16 g.
- Dietary fiber: 4 g.
- Total fat: 3 g.

Carrot and Potato Soup

Preparation time: 10 minutes
Cooking time: 30 minutes
Servings: 3

Ingredients
- 1 C. reduced-sodium vegetable stock
- ½ C. scallions, green tips only, sliced
- 2 medium potatoes, diced
- 2 large carrots, diced
- 1 ½ tbsp. fresh cilantro, chopped, plus more for garnishing
- ¼ C. almond milk

Directions
1. Bring 2 tbsps. stock to the boil in a deep pot.
2. Add the scallions and stir gently for 1–2 minutes.
3. Add the potatoes and carrots to the pot, and cook over low heat for 5 minutes, stirring occasionally.
4. Add the remaining stock to the saucepan and turn up the heat to bring the soup to a rolling boil.
5. Reduce the heat, cover, and simmer for 10–15 minutes until the vegetables are softened.
6. Remove the soup from the heat, and add in the fresh cilantro.
7. Set the soup aside to cool. When the soup is cool enough to handle, blend with a handheld blender until the soup reaches your desired consistency.
8. Return the soup to low heat and stir in the almond milk.
9. Serve warm topped with fresh cilantro.

Nutrition
- Calories: 145 kcal.
- Protein: 6 g.
- Total carbs: 28 g.
- Dietary fiber: 4 g.

Total fat: 2 g.

Red Pepper and Tomato Soup

Preparation time: 10 minutes
Cooking time: 40 minutes
Servings: 3

Ingredients
- 2 red peppers, deseeded and cut into strips
- 2 large carrots peeled and chopped
- 1 tbsp. rice bran oil
- 1 tsp. freshly ground black pepper, to taste
- 1 C. low-fat vegetable stock
- 1 C. canned tomatoes, chopped
- 3 tbsps. fresh parsley

Directions
1. Preheat the oven to 400°F.
2. Toss the peppers and carrots with the rice bran oil, and arrange them across an oven tray.
3. Season well with freshly ground black pepper.
4. Roast the vegetables for 20–25 minutes, being sure to stir the vegetables halfway through cooking. Transfer the vegetables with their juices into a deep soup pot.
5. Add the vegetable stock and the canned tomatoes to the pot. Blend with a handheld blender.
6. Bring the soup to a gentle boil to blend the flavors, and serve warm topped with fresh parsley.

Nutrition
- Calories: 54 kcal.
- Protein: 6 g.
- Total carbs: 8 g.
- Dietary fiber: 3 g.
- Total fat: 1 g.

Slow Cooker Chicken Soup With Baby Spinach Leaves

Preparation time: 10 minutes
Cooking time: 30 minutes
Servings: 3

Ingredients
- 2 C. low-fat chicken stock
- 6 oz. skinless chicken breasts, thickly sliced
- 2 large carrots, peeled and diced
- ½ C. scallions, green tips only, chopped
- ½ tsp. dried thyme
- ½ tsp. dried rosemary
- 2 bay leaves
- 1 tbsp. lemon juice
- 1 tsp. freshly ground black pepper, to taste
- 1 C. baby spinach leaves

Directions
1. Pour the chicken stock into the slow cooker.
2. Arrange the remaining ingredients except for the baby spinach leaves into the slow cooker. Cook for 6–7 hours on low. To serve, top the soup with the baby spinach leaves.

Nutrition
- Calories: 172 kcal.
- Protein: 23 g.
- Total carbs: 9 g.
- Dietary fiber: 4 g.

Total fat: 5 g.

Thai Chicken Soup

Preparation time: 10 minutes
Cooking time: 20 minutes
Servings: 3

Ingredients
- 1 C. low-fat chicken stock
- 1 C. water
- 6 oz. skinless chicken breasts, sliced
- 1 tsp. freshly ground black pepper, to taste
- ½ tsp. turmeric
- ½ tbsp. galangal, sliced
- 1 clove garlic, crushed

- 1 tbsp. sliced scallions, green ends only
- 1 large tomato, diced
- ⅓ C. baby corn
- ⅓ C. snow peas
- Juice of 1 lime

Directions
1. Combine the chicken stock and water in a soup pot and boil over high heat.
2. Reduce the heat, and add all the remaining ingredients, except for the snow peas and lime juice.
3. Bring to a boil again, then reduce the heat so that the soup is simmering for about 20–25 minutes.
4. Add the snow peas in the last 10 minutes of the cooking time. The soup is ready when the chicken is cooked through.
5. Stir in the lime juice, and serve warm.

Nutrition
- Calories: 166 kcal.
- Protein: 23 g.
- Total carbs: 13 g.
- Dietary fiber: 3 g.
- Total fat: 4 g.

Cumin and Turmeric Fish Stew

Preparation time: 10 minutes
Cooking time: 30 minutes
Servings: 3

Ingredients
- 1 tsp. olive oil cooking spray
- 1 tsp. grated fresh ginger
- 1 tsp. ground cumin
- 1 tsp. turmeric
- 1 tsp. cayenne pepper
- 1 C. cherry tomatoes
- 9 oz. water
- 6 oz. firm white fish fillets, cod, snapper, or ling, cut into chunks
- 1 tsp. freshly ground black pepper
- 1 tbsp. fresh cilantro leaves

Directions
1. Lightly spray a large heavy-based pot with the cooking spray, and heat over medium heat. Gently fry the ginger, cumin, and turmeric for about 2 minutes until the flavors are released.
2. Add the cayenne pepper, tomatoes, and water to the pot, and bring to a boil.
3. Reduce the heat, and simmer for 10–15 minutes.
4. Add the fish chunks to the soup and simmer for 5 minutes, or until the fish is almost cooked through and tender.
5. Season to taste with freshly ground black pepper and garnish with fresh cilantro leaves.

Nutrition
- Calories: 128 kcal.
- Protein: 16 g.
- Total carbs: 10 g.
- Dietary fiber: 5 g.
- Total fat: 4 g.

Cabbage Soup With Arugula Leaves

Preparation time: 10 minutes
Cooking time: 40 minutes
Servings: 3
Ingredients

- 1 tsp. olive oil cooking spray
- ¼ large onion, diced
- ½ clove garlic, minced
- 1 C. reduced-sodium chicken stock
- 1 head of cabbage, chopped
- 1 C. cherry tomatoes
- 7 fl oz. canned cannellini beans
- 2 C. arugula leaves

Directions

1. Lightly spray a large soup pot with cooking spray and heat over medium heat.
2. Add the onions and garlic to the pot, and sauté until their fragrances are released.
3. Add the chicken stock, cabbage, and tomatoes to the pot.
4. Add more water if necessary to just about cover the cabbage.
5. Bring to a boil, reduce the heat, and simmer until the cabbage is tender about 30 minutes.
6. Add the cannellini beans, and simmer for another 10 minutes.
7. Serve topped with fresh arugula leaves.

Nutrition

- Calories: 128 kcal.
- Protein: 8 g.
- Total carbs: 17 g.
- Dietary fiber: 10 g.

Total fat: 0 g.

Turkey Goulash With Baby Spinach Leaves

Preparation time: 10 minutes
Cooking time: 30 minutes
Servings: 3
Ingredients

- Olive oil cooking spray
- 6 oz. skinless turkey breast, cubed
- 1 carrot, diced
- ½ C. green pepper, chopped
- 4 beef tomatoes, chopped
- 1 tsp. paprika
- 1 tsp. freshly ground black pepper
- 1 tbsp. reduced-sodium tomato paste
- 1 C. reduced-sodium chicken stock
- 1 C. organic baby spinach leaves
- 1 tbsp. chives snipped

Directions

1. Lightly spray a nonstick frying pan with the olive oil cooking spray and heat on medium heat.
2. Add the turkey pieces and sear until they are evenly browned.
3. Add the carrot, pepper, tomatoes, paprika, and freshly ground black pepper.
4. Cook for 2 minutes and add the tomato paste and stock to the pan.
5. Bring to a boil, and then reduce the heat.
6. Cover the goulash with a lid, and simmer for 20 minutes until the sauce is thick and the flavors are well blended.
7. Stir occasionally to prevent the sauce from sticking to the pan.
8. Serve hot topped with the baby spinach leaves and freshly snipped chives.

Nutrition

- Calories: 210 kcal.
- Protein: 30 g.
- Total carbs: 20 g.
- Dietary fiber: 3 g.

Total fat: 4 g.

Carrot and Turkey Soup

Preparation time: 10 minutes
Cooking time: 30 minutes
Servings: 3
Ingredients

- 2 C. reduced-sodium chicken stock
- 6 oz. turkey breast, cubed

- 1 carrot, diced
- 1 cob of corn, cut into 2-inch-thick pieces
- 1 tbsp. fresh parsley roughly chopped

Directions
1. Bring the chicken stock to a boil in a soup pot over high heat.
2. Reduce the heat, and add the turkey, carrots, and corn pieces to the pot.
3. Ensure that the ingredients are submerged in the stock, and add some water to the pot if necessary.
4. Bring to a boil again, then reduce the heat, and simmer for 15–20 minutes until the turkey is cooked through.
5. Remove the turkey from the soup and set it aside to cool. When the turkey is cool enough to handle, shred the meat and return to pot with all its released juices.
6. Stir through.
7. Serve the soup warm, topped with fresh parsley.

Nutrition
- Calories: 177 kcal.
- Protein: 24 g.
- Total carbs: 15 g.
- Dietary fiber: 1 g.

Total fat: 4 g.

Fennel and Ginger Chicken Soup With Asparagus Tips

Preparation time: 10 minutes
Cooking time: 30 minutes
Servings: 3

Ingredients
- 2 small skinless chicken breasts, diced
- ¼ tsp. ground black pepper
- 1 bulb fennel, cored and cut into thin wedges
- 1 red bell pepper, deseeded, and diced
- 1 tsp. dried rosemary
- 1 tsp. ground ginger
- ½ C. reduced-sodium chicken stock
- ½ C. water
- 1 tbsp. dried oregano
- 7 oz. asparagus tips, not stalks

Directions
1. Season the chicken pieces with ground pepper and place them in the slow cooker pot.
2. Add the remaining ingredients to the pot.
3. Cover and cook on high for 2 ½–3 hours.

Nutrition
- Calories: 121 kcal.
- Protein: 19 g.
- Total carbs: 7 g.
- Dietary fiber: 3 g.

Total fat: 5 g.

Spinach Veal Broth

Preparation time: 15 minutes
Cooking time: 1 hour 10 minutes
Servings: 4
Ingredients:
1 lb veal steak, cut into bite-sized pieces
1 lb fresh spinach, torn
3 large eggs, beaten
4 cups vegetable broth
1 small onion, finely chopped
2 garlic cloves
3 tbsp extra-virgin olive oil
1 tsp salt
Directions:
Wash the meat under cold running water and pat dry with kitchen paper. Cut into bite-sized pieces and place in a medium bowl. Generously sprinkle with salt and pepper and stir well with your hands. Set aside.

Rinse spinach thoroughly and drain. Cut into bite-sized pieces and set aside.

Preheat the oil in a large skillet over medium-high temperature. Add meat and cook for 5 minutes, stirring occasionally. Add garlic and onions and give it a good stir. Cook for another 3-4 minutes, or until the onions are translucent.

Now, add vegetable broth and spinach. Bring it to a boil and then whisk in the eggs. Reduce the heat to low and cook for about an hour. Remove from the heat. Using a large sieve, remove the meat and vegetables from the liquid.

Add some salt if needed and pour the broth to a serving glass.

Enjoy!

Nutrition: Calories: 416, Protein: 43g, Total Carbs: 7.5g, Dietary Fibers: 2.9g, Total Fat: 23.9g

- **Carrot Lentil Broth**

Preparation time: 10 minutes
Cooking time: 25 minutes
Servings: 3
Ingredients:
1 cup red lentils, soaked overnight
4 large carrots, peeled and chopped
1 medium-sized onion, peeled and finely chopped
3 tbsp milk
1 tbsp all-purpose flour
½ tsp black pepper, freshly ground
½ tsp cumin, ground
½ tsp salt
2 tbsp olive oil
Directions:
Wash and peel the carrots. Place them in a food processor and add milk. Blend until smooth and creamy. Set aside.

After soaking the lentils overnight, rinse well and drain. Place in a deep pot of boiling water and cook for 15 minutes. Remove from the heat and drain. Set aside.

Preheat the oil in a large saucepan over a medium-high temperature. Add onions and flour. Stir-fry for 5 minutes, or until translucent.

Now, add carrot puree and lentils. Sprinkle with salt and pepper to taste and stir well. Cook for 1 minute and then add 4 cups of water. Stir well and bring it to a boil. Reduce the heat to low and cook for 1 hour. Remove from the heat.

Drain the liquid into a separate bowl and serve immediately.

Nutrition information per serving: Calories: 228, Protein: 11.1g, Total Carbs: 32.7g, Dietary Fibers: 13.7g, Total Fat: 6.3g

Celery Spinach Broth

Preparation time: 15 minutes
Cooking time: 45 minutes
Servings: 6
Ingredients:
1 lb fresh celery, chopped
1 lb fresh spinach, chopped
1 medium-sized red onion, finely chopped
1 cup heavy cream
1 cup water
1 cup sour cream
2 cups vegetable broth
2 tbsp butter
½ tsp dried thyme, ground
½ tsp salt
½ tsp black pepper, ground

Directions:

Combine celery and spinach in a large colander. Wash thoroughly under cold running water. Drain and chop into small pieces. Set aside.

Melt the butter in a large saucepan over medium-high temperature. Add onions and stir-fry until translucent. Add celery and spinach. Sprinkle with salt, thyme and pepper. Stir well and cook for about 3-4 minutes, or until celery and spinach are tender.

Add the vegetable broth and water. Stir well and bring it to a boil. Reduce the heat to low and cover with a lid. Cook for 15-20 minutes and then stir in the heavy cream and sour cream. Cook for another 5 minutes and remove from the heat.

Cover with a lid and cook for 20 minutes. Remove from the heat and stir in the heavy cream. Using a large sieve, separate the vegetables from the broth. Let it cool for a while and store in a glass jars.

Refrigerate up to 2 days or serve immediately.

Nutrition: Calories: 235, Protein: 6.2g, Total Carbs: 9.4g, Dietary Fibers: 3.3g, Total Fat: 20.2g

Carrot Coconut Broth

Preparation time: 15 minutes
Cooking time: 20 minutes
Servings: 6
Ingredients:
6 large carrots, thinly sliced
2 cups coconut milk
1 medium-sized sweet potato, chopped
1 small onion, chopped
2 cups chicken broth
1 tsp curry powder
2 garlic cloves, crushed
1 tbsp vegetable oil
1 tsp salt
¼ tsp black pepper, ground
Directions:
Preheat the oil in a deep pot over a medium-high temperature. Add onions and stir-fry them until translucent. Add garlic and mix well with onions. Cook for another minute.

Add carrots, potatoes, and chicken broth. Bring it to a boil and sprinkle with curry, salt, and pepper. Cook for 15 minutes and then add coconut milk. Cook until heated through and remove from the heat.

Now, separate the broth and vegetables. Store the broth into a glass jars and refrigerate up to 2 days.

Nutrition: Calories: 271, Protein: 4.7g, Total Carbs: 17.4g, Dietary Fibers: 4.6g, Total Fat: 21.9g

Eggplant Tomato Soup

Preparation time: 10 minutes
Cooking time: 20 minutes
Servings: 4
Ingredients:
2 medium-sized eggplants, peeled and cubed
2 large tomatoes, peeled and diced
1 medium-sized red onion, finely chopped
2 tbsp olive oil
1 tsp salt
½ tsp black pepper, ground
½ cup sour cream
½ tsp dried oregano, ground
Directions:
Peel the eggplants and cut into small cubes. Set aside. Wash and peel the tomatoes. Chop into small pieces and set aside.

Preheat the oil in a large skillet over medium-high temperature. Add onions and stir-fry for 3 minutes, and then add eggplants. Stir well and cook for 5 minutes. Add diced tomatoes and stir well. Pour 1 cup of water and bring it to a boil, stirring occasionally.

Remove from the heat and set aside to cool. Transfer to a food processor in batches. Blend until nicely pureed.

Return to the pot and add about 3 cups of water. Bring it to a boil and then stir in the sour cream and oregano. Cook until heated through and remove from the heat.

Serve warm.

Nutrition information per serving: Calories: 207, Protein: 4.3g, Total Carbs: 21.1g, Dietary Fibers: 9.9g, Total Fat: 13.7g

- **Sage Soup**

Preparation time: 5 minutes
Cooking time: 30 minutes
Servings: 4
Ingredients:
2 cups fresh sage, roughly chopped
1 medium-sized onion, finely chopped
1 tbsp all-purpose flour
1 cup bone broth
1 tsp cayenne pepper, ground
½ tsp garlic powder
2 tbsp olive oil
½ cup sour cream
Directions:
Wash the sage thoroughly under cold running water. Drain well and place in deep pot. Add enough water to cover and bring it to a boil. Cook for 1 minute and remove from the heat and drain well. Set aside.
Preheat the oil in a large skillet over medium-high temperature. Add onion and stir-fry for 3 minutes, or until translucent. Add flour, garlic, and ½ cup of water. Reduce the heat to low and simmer for 2 more minutes. Add broth and 1 cup of water. Bring it to a boil and then add sage. Cook for 15 minutes and then remove from the heat. Let it cool for a while.
Transfer all to a food processor and pulse until creamy. Return to the pot and stir in the sour cream.
Serve immediately.
Nutrition information per serving: Calories: 214, Protein: 8.2g, Total Carbs: 15.5g, Dietary Fibers: 7.2g, Total Fat: 15.2g

Acorn Squash Cream Soup

Preparation time: 15 minutes
Cooking time: 1 hour 5 minutes
Servings: 6
Ingredients:
2 medium-sized acorn squash
4 cups chicken broth
3 garlic cloves, finely chopped
3 tbsp olive oil
2 tbsp lime juice, freshly squeezed
1 medium-sized onion, roughly chopped
½ cup sour cream
1 tsp black pepper, ground
½ tsp salt
Directions:
Preheat the oven to 350°F.
Cut the squash lengthwise in half and scoop out the seeds. Place it on a large baking sheet and set aside.
Peel the onion and cut into large pieces. Spread evenly over the squash.
In a small bowl, combine olive oil and garlic. Drizzle over the squash. Place it in the oven and bake for about 40-45 minutes, or until nicely tender. Remove from the oven and allow it to cool completely.
Now, transfer all to a large saucepan and add the remaining ingredients.
Cover with a lid and cook for 15 minutes on low temperature. Transfer to a food processor and blend until smooth and creamy.
Stir in the sour cream and reheat. Sprinkle with some more salt and pepper if you like. However, it's optional. Serve warm.
Nutrition: Calories: 195, Protein: 5.3g, Total Carbs: 18.8g, Dietary Fibers: 2.7g, Total Fat: 12.1g

- **Creamy Leek Soup**

Preparation time: 15 minutes
Cooking time: 20 minutes
Servings: 3
Ingredients:
1 cup leeks, chopped
1 medium-sized potato
1 large carrot, chopped
1 cup chicken stock, unsalted
1 cup milk, low-fat
1 cup spinach, finely chopped
1 tbsp parsley, finely chopped
¼ tsp black pepper, ground
Directions:
Wash and prepare the vegetables. Place the leeks, spinach, and celery in a pot of boiling water. Cook for 3 minutes and remove from the heat. Drain well and set aside.
Place the potato in a pot of boiling water and cook for 5 minutes, or until slightly tender. Remove from the heat and drain well. Set aside.

Now, combine leeks, potato, carrot, and spinach in a heavy-bottomed pot. Pour the chicken stock and milk. Sprinkle with pepper and parsley. Bring it to a boil and then reduce the heat to low. Simmer for 15 minutes and remove from the heat. Transfer all to a food processor and pulse until creamy and pureed. Return to the pot and reheat.

Serve warm.

Nutrition: Calories: 130, Protein: 5.3g, Total Carbs: 23.8g, Dietary Fibers: 3g, Total Fat: 2.1g

Green Cream Soup

Preparation time: 5 minutes
Cooking time: 15 minutes
Servings: 2
Ingredients:
1 cup fresh broccoli, chopped
1 cup cauliflower, chopped
4 tbsp fresh parsley, finely chopped
¼ tsp chili pepper, ground
1 tsp dried thyme, ground
½ cup milk, low-fat
Directions:
Place broccoli and cauliflower in a heavy-bottomed pot. Add enough water to cover all ingredients and bring it to a boil. Cook for 5 minutes, or until tender. Remove from the heat and drain well. Set aside to cool for a while.

Transfer cooked broccoli and cauliflower to a blender. Add ½ cup of water and sprinkle with chili pepper. Process until pureed and transfer to a clean heavy-bottomed pot.

Add 2 cups of water and sprinkle with finely chopped parsley. Bring to a boil and reduce the heat to low. Cook for 2 minutes. Add milk and give it a good stir. Cook for five more minutes over medium-high heat.

Serve warm.

Nutrition: Calories: 63, Protein: 4.6g, Total Carbs: 9.5g, Dietary Fibers: 2.9g, Total Fat: 1.6g

Spinach Potato Cream Soup

Preparation time: 15 minutes
Cooking time: 35 minutes
Servings: 6
Ingredients:
1 lb fresh spinach, chopped
2 medium-sized potatoes, chopped
3 tbsp fresh parsley, chopped
1 small onion, finely chopped
2 tbsp olive oil
2 tbsp all-purpose flour
2 cups chicken broth
1 cup cream cheese
½ tsp cayenne pepper
1 tsp salt
¼ tsp black pepper, ground
Directions:
Rinse the spinach thoroughly under cold running water. Drain well and chop into small pieces. Set aside.

Peel the potatoes and chop into bite-sized pieces. Set aside.

Place the spinach in a pot of boiling water and cook for 3 minutes, or until tender. Remove from the heat and drain. Set aside.

Place the potatoes in a pot of boiling water and sprinkle with some salt. Bring it to a boil and cook for 10 minutes. Remove from the heat and drain. Set aside.

Preheat the oil in a large skillet over a medium-high temperature. Add onion and stir-fry until translucent. Stir in the flour, cayenne pepper, and 1 tablespoon of water. Cook for 1 minute, stirring constantly. Remove from the heat.

In a large heavy-bottomed pot, pour chicken broth and 1 cup of water. Bring it to a boil over a medium-high temperature.

Add spinach and potatoes and sprinkle with pepper. Cook for 10 minutes, and reduce heat to low. Cook for another 5 minutes and then stir in the sour cream and parsley.

Now, transfer all to a food processor in few batches. Pulse until creamy and pureed. Transfer to the pot and stir in the flour mixture. Cook for 2 more minutes.

Remove from the heat and set aside to cool for a while before serving.

Nutrition: Calories: 270, Protein: 8.4g, Total Carbs: 18.6g, Dietary Fibers: 3.8g, Total Fat: 19.1g

Chicken Cauliflower Soup

Preparation time: 10 minutes
Cooking time: 25 minutes
Servings: 4
Ingredients:
10 oz chicken fillets, cut into bite-sized pieces
1 cup cauliflower, chopped
1 tsp fresh mint, finely chopped
¼ tsp dry coriander, crushed
1 tbsp olive oil
½ tsp salt
¼ tsp black pepper
Directions:
Wash the cauliflower thoroughly and remove the outer leaves. Cut into small pieces and fill the measuring cup. Reserve the rest in the refrigerator.
Place the cauliflower and dry coriander into a deep pot. Add enough water to cover and bring it to a boil. Cook for about 10-15 minutes. Remove from the heat and blend the soup with a stick blender. Set aside.
Now, preheat the oil in a large skillet over a medium-high temperature. Add meat chops and sprinkle with some salt and pepper. Cook for 5-8 minutes, or until golden brown. Remove from the heat and add it to the soup.
Now, transfer all to a food processor. Pulse until creamy and well combined. Return the soup to the pot and reheat.
Garnish with fresh mint before serving and enjoy!
Nutrition: Calories: 171, Protein: 21g, Total Carbs: 1.5g, Dietary Fibers: 0.7g, Total Fat: 8.8g

Zucchini Cream Soup

Preparation time: 10 minutes
Cooking time: 40 minutes
Servings: 3
Ingredients:
1 lb zucchini, chopped
3 cups vegetable broth
1 small onion, chopped
2 cups milk, low-fat
4 tbsp Greek yogurt
1 tsp fresh sage, finely chopped
1 garlic clove, crushed
1 tsp olive oil
½ tsp salt
¼ tsp black pepper, ground
Directions:
Peel the zucchinis and chop into bite-sized pieces. Set aside.
Peel the onion and chop into small pieces. Set aside.
Preheat the oil in a heavy-bottomed pot over medium-high temperature. Add onion and garlic and stir-fry until translucent.
Now, add the zucchini chops and sprinkle with some sage to taste. Pour the vegetable broth and stir all well. Bring it to a boil and then reduce the heat to low. Cover with a lid and cook for about 25-30 minutes more. Remove from the heat and set aside to cool for a while.
Transfer all to the food processor and blend until creamy. Now, return to the pot and heat up. Sprinkle with salt and pepper and remove from the heat.
Stir in the Greek yogurt and milk.
Serve warm.
Nutrition: Calories: 162, Protein: 15.5g, Total Carbs: 13.3g, Dietary Fibers: 1.4g, Total Fat: 5.6g

Broccoli Gorgonzola Soup

Preparation time: 10 minutes
Cooking time: 2 hours
Servings: 6
Ingredients:
10 oz Gorgonzola cheese, crumbled
1 cup broccoli, finely chopped
1 tbsp olive oil
½ cup full-fat milk
½ cup vegetable broth
1 tbsp parsley, finely chopped
½ tsp salt
¼ tsp black pepper, ground
Directions:
Wash the broccoli under cold running water. Drain and chop into bite-sized pieces. Set aside.
Grease the bottom of a deep pot with olive oil. Add all ingredients and three cups of water. Mix well with a kitchen whisker until fully combined.
Cover with a lid and cook for 2 hours on low temperature.

Remove from the heat and sprinkle with some fresh parsley for extra taste.

I like to stir in one tablespoon of Greek yogurt before serving, but it's optional.

Nutrition: Calories: 204, Protein: 11.9g, Total Carbs: 5.1g, Dietary Fibers: 1.9g, Total Fat: 16.5g

Chickpea Pepper Soup

Preparation time: 5 minutes
Cooking time: 40 minutes
Servings: 4
Ingredients:
14 oz chickpeas, soaked
2 large red bell peppers, finely chopped
2 small onions, peeled and finely chopped
2 large tomatoes, peeled and finely chopped
3 tbsp tomato paste
Handful fresh parsley, finely chopped
2 cups vegetable broth
3 tbsp extra virgin olive oil
1 tsp sat
Directions:

Soak the chickpeas overnight. Rinse and drain. Place the chickpeas in a pot of boiling water and cook for 30 minutes. Remove from the heat and drain. Set aside.

Wash the bell pepper and cut lengthwise in half. Remove the seeds and finely chop it. Set aside.

Preheat the oil in a large saucepan over medium-high temperature. Add onions and bell peppers. Cook for 5 minutes, or until tender. Add tomatoes, tomato paste, and parsley. Stir well and cook for 2 minutes. Now, add chickpeas and broth. Sprinkle with salt and stir again. Bring it to a boil and reduce the heat to low. Cook for 30 minutes and remove from the heat.

Serve warm.

Nutrition: Calories: 353, Protein: 15.9g, Total Carbs: 49.5g, Dietary Fibers: 13.6g, Total Fat: 11.7g

Fresh Tomato and Celery Soup

Preparation time: 10 minutes
Cooking time: 30 minutes
Servings: 4
Ingredients:
1 lb tomatoes, peeled and roughly chopped
3.5 oz celery root, finely chopped
¼ cup fresh celery leaves, finely chopped
1 tbsp fresh basil, finely chopped
Salt and pepper to taste
5 tbsp extra virgin olive oil
Directions:

Preheat the oil in a large non-stick frying pan over a medium-high temperature. Add finely chopped celery root, celery leaves, and fresh basil. Season with salt and pepper and stir-fry for about 10 minutes, until nicely browned.

Add chopped tomatoes and about ¼ cup of water. Reduce the heat to minimum and cook for 15 minutes, stirring constantly, until softened. Now add about 4 cups of water (or vegetable broth) and bring it to a boil. Give it a good stir and remove from the heat.

Top with fresh parsley and serve.

Nutrition: Kcal: 122, Protein: 1.4g, Total Carbs: 6.9g, Dietary Fibers: 1.9g, Total Fats: 10.8g

Creamy Wild Asparagus Soup

Preparation time: 10 minutes
Cooking time: 20 minutes
Servings: 6
Ingredients:
2 lbs fresh wild asparagus, trimmed
2 small onions, peeled and finely chopped
1 cup heavy cream
4 cups of vegetable broth
2 tbsp butter
1 tbsp vegetable oil
½ tsp salt
½ tsp dried oregano
½ tsp cayenne pepper
Directions:
Rinse and drain asparagus. Cut into about one-inch thick pieces. Set aside.
Melt the butter in a large skillet and add oil. Heat up and add onions. Cook until translucent.
Now add trimmed asparagus, oregano, salt, and cayenne pepper. Stir well and continue to cook until asparagus soften.
Add the vegetable broth and mix well to combine. Cook for 15 minutes, stirring occasionally.
Whisk in one cup of heavy cream and serve.
Nutrition: Kcal: 189, Protein: 7.3g, Total Carbs: 9.4g, Dietary Fibers: 3.8g, Total Fats: 14.7g

• Homemade Chicken Soup

Preparation time: 20 minutes
Cooking time: 40 minutes
Servings: 4
Ingredients:
1 lb chicken meat
½ cup soup noodles
4 cups chicken broth
A handful fresh parsley
1 tsp salt
¼ tsp freshly ground black pepper
Directions:
For this recipe, I always try to find an organic chicken. They are much tastier and better for a homemade soup. Use both dark and white pieces and rinse well under the running water. Pat dry with kitchen paper and place on a clean work surface.
Using a sharp paring knife, cut chicken into bite-sized pieces. Sprinkle with salt and place in a deep pot. If using organic chicken, be careful not to add extra fat because this meat already has enough fat.
Pour in the chicken broth and cover with a lid. Cook for 45 minutes, over medium-high heat.
Now add soup noodles and reduce the heat to minimum. Cook for five more minutes.
Sprinkle with some freshly ground black pepper and parsley.
Serve warm.
Nutrition: Kcal: 267, Protein: 38.5g, Total Carbs: 2.8g, Dietary Fibers: 0.6g, Total Fats: 10.2g

• Butternut Squash Soup

Preparation Time: 10 minutes
Cooking Time: 40 minutes
Servings: 4-6
Ingredients:
2 tablespoons olive oil
2/3 cup onions, finely chopped
1 cup carrots, thinly sliced
1 large potato, peeled, cubed
2 cups butternut squash, peeled, cubed
1 Granny Smith apple, peeled, cored, cubed
4 cups chicken broth
¼ teaspoon nutmeg
salt and pepper to taste
½ cup milk (optional)
Directions:
In a medium saucepan, heat olive oil; add onions and cook over low heat until softened, about 5 minutes.
Add carrots, potato, squash, apple, and chicken broth; cover and cook over low heat until vegetables are tender, about 30 minutes. Stir in nutmeg, salt and pepper.
Place half the mixture into a blender; blend until smooth. Pour into another saucepan or large bowl and blend the remaining half of the vegetables until smooth.
Return to saucepan; stir in milk if desired. Serve.
Nutrition:
Calories 100
Total Fat 2.5g

Total Carbohydrate 20g
Protein 2g

Simple Meatball Soup

Preparation Time: 10 minutes
Cooking Time: 1 hour
Servings: 4-6
Ingredients:
2 teaspoons olive oil
1 small onion, finely chopped
2 cloves garlic, finely chopped
2 cups tomato juice
2 cups chicken broth
½ cup water
¾ cup vegetable juice blend (such as V8)
½ cup green pepper, finely chopped
1/3 cup white quinoa, uncooked
24 meatballs, prepackaged, frozen

Directions:
In a large saucepan, heat olive oil; add garlic and onion, and allow to cook on medium heat until soft, about 5 mins.

Add tomato juice, broth, water, vegetable juice, and green pepper; bring to near boiling then reduce heat.

Cover; cook over low heat 30 minutes, or until onions and peppers are soft and flavors are well blended; stir occasionally.

Add quinoa and meatballs; cover and continue cooking for 25 minutes, or until quinoa is tender and meatballs are heated throughout.

Nutrition:
Calories 277
Total Fat 14g
Total Carbohydrate 26 g
Protein 13g

Chicken Barley Soup

Preparation Time: 10 minutes
Cooking Time: 1 hour
Servings: 6-8
Ingredients:
1-pound ground chicken
2 (14-ounce) cans chicken broth
1 cup vegetable juice blend (such as V8)
4 cups water
1 cup carrots, peeled and thinly sliced
½ cup cabbage, finely shredded
½ cup green pepper, diced
1 cup onion, finely chopped
2 cloves garlic, minced
2 teaspoons seasoned salt
¾ cup barley, uncooked

Directions:
In a large saucepan, cook ground chicken, stirring until ground chicken is browned and crumbly. Drain fat

Add broth, juice, water, carrots, cabbage, green pepper, onion, garlic, seasoned salt and barley; stir.

Cover; cook over low heat for 1½-2 hours, or until barley is tender; stir occasionally.

Nutrition:
Calories 90
Total Fat 3g
Total Carbohydrate 11 g
Protein 5g

Ham and Bean Soup

Preparation Time: 10 minutes
Cooking Time: 5 hours
Servings: 8
Ingredients:
½ (16-ounce) package navy beans
(14-ounce) cans chicken broth
2 cups water
1 cup carrots, thinly sliced
1 cup onion, finely chopped
2 cloves garlic, sliced
1 (14-ounce) can diced tomatoes, with juice
½ teaspoon black pepper
1½ teaspoons seasoned salt
1 cup green cabbage, finely chopped
1 (5-ounce) can smoked ground ham
Directions:
Wash navy beans according to package directions.
In a large saucepan, heat 1-quart water to boiling. Remove from heat; add beans, cover and let sit for one hour to soften; drain.
Add broth, water, carrots, onion, garlic, tomatoes, pepper, seasoned salt, cabbage, and ham. Cover; cook on low heat for 3-4 hours, or until beans become very soft. Stir occasionally.
Using a potato masher, mash beans until about half of them are broken apart; stir to blend.
Nutrition:
Calories 177
Total Fat 2g
Total Carbohydrate 26g
Protein 14g

French Onion Soup

Preparation Time: 10 minutes
Cooking Time: 40 minutes
Servings: 6
Ingredients:
1 tablespoon olive oil
2 cups sweet onions, finely chopped
4 cups chicken broth
½ cup dry red wine
1 teaspoon garlic, finely chopped
6 slices French bread, 1-inch thick
6 tablespoons Parmesan cheese, freshly grated
Directions:
In a large saucepan, add olive oil and onions; cook over medium heat, stirring often, until onions are browned.
Add broth, wine, and garlic; cover and cook over low heat for 25 minutes.
Meanwhile, toast bread until lightly browned; place one piece of toast in bottom of individual soup bowls; sprinkle each toast with 1 tablespoon Parmesan cheese.
Pour soup over toast to serve.
Nutrition:
Calories 190
Total Fat 9g
Total Carbohydrate 21g
Protein 7g

Cheesy Cauliflower Soup

Preparation Time: 10 minutes
Cooking Time: 45 minutes
Servings: 6-8
Ingredients:
3 tablespoons olive oil
3/4 cup onions, finely chopped
5 cups chicken broth
1 cup water
1 medium cauliflower, cut into florets
1/3 teaspoon rosemary
1/8 teaspoon thyme
¼ teaspoon black pepper
2 tablespoons butter, melted
¼ cup whole flour
2 cups cheddar cheese, shredded
Directions:
In a large saucepan, heat oil; add onions and cook over medium heat until softened, about 5 minutes.
Add broth, water, cauliflower, rosemary, thyme, and pepper. Cover; cook over low heat for 30 minutes, or until cauliflower is tender. Remove from heat.
Using a potato masher, mash cauliflower mixture until cauliflower is broken into small pieces; return to heat.
In a small bowl, combine melted butter and flour; mix well, then add to soup, cooking over low heat and stirring until soup is thickened to desired consistency.

Add cheese, one cup at a time, stirring until cheese is melted. Serve.
Nutrition:
Calories 252
Total Fat 14g
Total Carbohydrate 24g
Protein 0g

• Creamy Chicken Vegetable Soup

Preparation Time: 15 minutes
Cooking Time: 45 minutes
Servings: 6
Ingredients:
2 tablespoons olive oil
½ cup onions, finely chopped
½ cup carrots, thinly sliced or shredded
½ cup potatoes, diced
½ cup green beans
½ cup peas
1 cup chicken, finely chopped
1 (14-ounce) can chicken broth
¼ teaspoon black pepper
1¼ cups milk
1 (10¾-ounce) can cream of celery soup
1 (10¾-ounce) can cream of cheddar cheese soup
Directions:
In a large saucepan, heat oil; add onions and carrots; cook and stir until softened, about 5 minutes.
Add potatoes, green beans, peas, chicken, broth, and pepper. Cover, and cook over low heat for 1½ hours, or until vegetables are soft; stir occasionally.
Add milk, celery soup and cheddar cheese soup; stir and continue cooking until heated throughout.
Nutrition:
Calories 125
Total Fat 3.6g
Total Carbohydrate 15.6g
Protein 7.6g

• Clam Chowder

Preparation Time: 10 minutes
Cooking Time: 45 minutes
Servings: 6
Ingredients:
1 cup onion, finely chopped
3 cups potatoes, diced
1 clove garlic, finely chopped
2 slices turkey bacon, cooked and finely crumbled
1 teaspoon salt
¼ teaspoon black pepper
1 (8-ounce) bottle clam juice
2 (7-ounce) cans minced clams
3 tablespoons whole flour
1 cup milk
2 cups half-and-half
Directions:
Remove starch from potatoes by slicing them and soaking in lukewarm water and straining 4 times.
In a large saucepan, combine onion, potatoes, garlic, turkey bacon, salt, pepper, and clam juice; cover and cook on low for 30 minutes, or until vegetables are soft.
In a small bowl, stir flour into milk; mix well.
Add flour and milk mixture to saucepan along with half-and-half and clams with their liquid; stirring constantly, cook over medium heat until chowder thickens to desired consistency.
Transfer the mixture to a blender; blend until smooth and return to saucepan.
Nutrition:
Calories 163
Total Fat 5.83g
Total Carbohydrate 19.01g
Protein 8.83g

Cream of Broccoli Soup

Preparation Time: 10 minutes
Cooking Time: 45 minutes
Servings: 6
Ingredients:
4 cups broccoli florets
1 cup onion, chopped
1 tablespoon celery flakes
1 clove garlic, chopped
1 medium potato, peeled and diced
1 (14-ounce) chicken broth
2 cups milk
1½ cups cheddar cheese, shredded
¼ teaspoon thyme
½ teaspoon salt
¼ teaspoon white pepper
Directions:
In a medium saucepan, add broccoli, onion, celery flakes, garlic, potato, and chicken broth; bring to near boiling; reduce heat, cover and cook over low heat for 30 minutes, or until vegetables are soft.
Transfer cooked vegetables with broth to a blender; blend until smooth.
Return blended vegetables to saucepan; add milk, cheese, thyme, salt, and pepper.
Continue cooking over low heat until cheese is melted, stirring constantly.
Nutrition:
Calories 150
Total Fat 7g
Total Carbohydrate 15g
Protein 5g

Chicken Noodle Soup

Preparation Time: 10 minutes
Cooking Time: 1 hour 30 minutes
Servings: 6-8
Ingredients:
1 tablespoon olive or canola oil
¾ cup onion, finely chopped
2/3 cup carrots, shredded
4 cups chicken broth
2 cups water
1 tablespoon dried celery flakes
1 bay leaf
1 cup cooked chicken, finely chopped
1 tablespoon parsley flakes
1 teaspoon seasoned salt
¼ teaspoon black pepper, or to taste
1½ cups egg noodles, uncooked and broken into 3-inch pieces
Directions:
In a large saucepan, add oil, carrots and onion then allow to cook on medium heat until soft, about 5 minutes.
Add broth, water, celery flakes, bay leaf, and chicken; cover and cook over low heat for 1 hour, stirring occasionally.
Stir in parsley, seasoned salt, pepper, and noodles; cover and continue cooking over low heat for 25 minutes. Remove bay leaf before serving.
Nutrition:
Calories 220
Total Fat 5g
Total Carbohydrate 24g
Protein 18g

Cream of Potato Soup

Preparation Time: 10 minutes
Cooking Time: 45 minutes
Servings: 6
Ingredients:
1 tablespoon butter
1 cup onion, finely chopped
3 cups diced potatoes
3 cups chicken broth
¼ teaspoon black pepper
½ teaspoon salt
½ teaspoon garlic powder
¼ cup whole flour
1½ cups milk
1 cup sharp cheddar cheese, shredded (optional)
Directions:
In a medium saucepan, melt butter over medium heat. Add onion; stir and cook until onions are softened.
Add potatoes, chicken broth, pepper, salt, and garlic powder, plus ham if desired.

Cover; cook over low heat until potatoes are tender and easily fall apart, about 40 minutes.

In a small bowl, combine flour and milk; mix until smooth. Stir flour mixture into soup; continue cooking and stirring until soup is thickened and of desired consistency.

Add cheese if desired; stir just until melted and smooth. Serve.

Nutrition:
Calories 225.7
Total Fat 5.7g
Total Carbohydrate 39g
Protein 4.6g

• *Chicken and Bean Soup*

Preparation Time: 10 minutes
Cooking Time: 40 minutes
Servings: 2-4
Ingredients:
1 tablespoon olive oil
½ cup onion, finely chopped
1 clove garlic, finely chopped
1 (14½-ounce) can chicken broth, with roasted vegetable and herb flavoring
½ cup water
1 cup canned great northern beans, rinsed and drained
¾ cup chicken, cooked and finely chopped
¼ teaspoon black pepper
1 strip veggie bacon, cooked and finely crumbled
Directions:
In a medium saucepan, heat oil; add onion and garlic, cooking over low heat until softened, about 5 minutes.
Add broth and water to saucepan; bring to near boiling; reduce heat.
Add remaining ingredients; cover and cook over low heat for 30 minutes. Stir occasionally.
Nutrition:
Calories 225.7
Total Fat 5.7g
Total Carbohydrate 39g
Protein 4.6g

• *Chicken Ramen Soup Broth*

Preparation Time: 10 minutes
Cooking Time: 1 hour
Servings: 2-3
Ingredients:
Onion, large, diced (1)
Carrots, diced (2)
Celery, diced (3)
Garlic, finely chopped (4 cloves)
Kosher salt (1 tsp)
Pepper (½ tsp)
Cinnamon (2 tsp)
Chicken broth, low sodium (6)
Light Miso (2 tsp)
Chicken breasts (1 lb.)
Spinach (1 bag)
Directions
Prepare carrots, celery, and onions for cooking in a latch Dutch oven for 5-7 minutes over medium heat. Now include salt, pepper, cinnamon, and garlic, and continue to cook for an additional minute.
Add chicken broth and miso before bringing to a boil.
Now add whole chicken breasts (raw), and simmer. Continue for 10-12 minutes. Occasionally remove a chicken breast and cut it, to see if it is cooked.
When the chicken is cooked thoroughly, relocate it to a cutting board for cooling.
When the chicken is cool enough to be handled, mince it finely, then add it back into the vegetable broth.
Stir in spinach to cook for approximately 5 minutes until spinach is tender.
Serve and enjoy!
Nutrition:
Calories 326.9
Total Fat 13.4 g
Total Carbohydrate 39.7 g
Protein 10.3 g

Carrot, Ginger Gusto Apple Soup

Preparation time: 15 minutes
Cooking Time: 35 minutes
Servings: 3
Ingredients:
2 cup yellow apple, chunks, peeled
1 cup boiled chicken, shredded
1 carrot, peeled and chopped
¼ cup cherries, chopped
2 cups chicken broth
1 tablespoons lemon juice
1 teaspoon ginger paste
½ teaspoon black pepper
¼ teaspoon salt
1 tablespoon oil
Directions
Heat oil in a pan, add ginger paste and fry for 1 minute.
Add all chicken and carrots, then fry well.
Season with salt and pepper.
Transfer apple chunks, strawberries, chicken broth and stir well.
Place to cook on low fire for 30 minutes.
Drizzle lemon juice.
Strain, and ladle into serving bowls.
Serve and enjoy.
Nutrition:
Calories 172.3
Total Fat 8.7 g
Total Carbohydrate 22.7 g
Protein 3.2 g

Carrot, Ginger Zest Chicken Orangey Soup 20

Preparation Time: 5 minutes
Cooking Time: 15 minutes
Servings: 3
Ingredients:
1 oz. chicken bones or boiled chicken feet
2 oranges, sliced, seeded
2 carrots, peeled and chopped
2 cups chicken broth
1 teaspoon ginger paste
½ teaspoon chili powder
¼ teaspoon salt
1 tablespoon oil
Directions
Heat oil in a pan, add ginger paste and carrot, then cook for 1 minute.
Add chicken, salt, chili powder and fry till golden brown.
Add chicken broth, orange slice and stir.
Leave to cook on low heat for 15 minutes.
Strain and ladle into serving bowls.
Serve and enjoy.
Nutrition:
Calories 159
Total Fat 3 g
Total Carbohydrate 27 g
Protein 6 g

Rice Cooker Garden soup

Preparation Time: 10 minutes
Cooking Time: 50 minutes
Servings: 6
Ingredients:
15oz. can chickpeas, rinsed and drained
2 carrots, diced
2 zucchinis, trimmed, cubed
2 sprigs thyme
1 leek, white and light green parts chopped
½ cup bulgur
4oz. green beans, cut into ½-inch pieces
6 cups water
2 garlic cloves, minced
2 cups chicken stock
2 tablespoons butter
1 cup tomatoes, chopped
1 cup fresh peas
1 bay leaf
Salt and pepper, to taste
Directions:
Set your rice cooker to white rice.
Add the butter and once melted add the celery, chickpeas, leek, garlic, zucchinis, garlic.
Cook, stirring for 4 minutes.
Add the stock, bulgur, tomatoes, bay leaf, water, and thyme.

Simmer for 30 minutes. Add the green beans and peas. Discard the thyme. Cook for 5 minutes. Serve after.
Nutrition:
Calories 100
Total Fat 3.5 g
Total Carbohydrate 18 g
Protein 3 g

• Lemony Chicken Soup Broth

Preparation Time: 10 minutes
Cooking Time: 1 hour
Servings: 2-3
Ingredients
Onion, large, diced (1)
Carrots, diced (2)
Celery, diced (3)
Garlic, finely chopped (4 cloves)
Kosher salt (1 tsp)
Pepper (½ tsp)
Cinnamon (2 tsp)
Chicken broth, low sodium (6)
Parsley, extra for garnish (10 sprigs)
Chicken breasts (1 lb.)
Spinach (1 bag)
Chick peas, canned, washed/ drained (15 ounces)
Juice of a Lemon (½ lemon, or more to taste)
Directions
Prepare carrots, celery, and onions for cooking in a latch Dutch oven for 5-7 minutes over medium heat. Now include salt, pepper, cinnamon, and garlic, and continue to cook for an additional minute.
Add whole parsley sprigs to your pot and stir in chicken broth before bringing to a boil.
Now add whole chicken breasts (raw), and simmer. Continue for 10-12 minutes. Occasionally remove a chicken breast and cut it, to see if it is cooked.
When the chicken is cooked thoroughly, relocate it to a cutting board for cooling.
When the chicken is cool enough to be handled, shred it, then add it back into the vegetable broth.
Stir in lemon juice, chick peas, and spinach to cook for approximately 5 minutes until spinach is tender.

Strain the soup to gather the broth and discard the solids, garnish with newly chopped parsley, and enjoy!
Nutrition:
Calories 252.8
Total Fat 8 g
Total Carbohydrate 19.8 g
Protein 25.6 g

Super Soup

Preparation Time: 10 minutes
Cooking Time: 30 minutes
Servings: 6
Ingredients:
14oz. cauliflower heat, cut into florets
5oz. watercress
7oz. spinach, thawed
4 cups chicken stock
1 cup coconut milk
¼ cup ghee
Salt and pepper – to taste
1 onion, chopped
2 garlic cloves, crushed
Directions:
Grease Dutch oven with ghee, place over medium-high heat and add onion and garlic. Cook until browned and stir cauliflower florets. Cook for 5 minutes.
Add spinach and water cress and cook for 2 minutes or until just wilted, pour in vegetable stock and bring to boil.
Cook until cauliflower is crisp-tender and stir in the coconut milk.
Season with salt and pepper and remove from the heat. Allow cooling and puree the soup in Nutri Bullet until creamy.
Strain through a fine sieve or cheesecloth and serve immediately.
Nutrition:
Calories 392
Total Fat 37.6 g
Total Carbohydrate 9.7 g
Protein 4.9 g

Tomato bisque

Preparation Time: 10 minutes
Cooking Time: 30 minutes
Servings: 4
Ingredients:
28oz. tomatoes, peeled and pureed
1 cup coconut cream
1 onion, diced
1 teaspoon fresh ground pepper
4 cups chicken stock
1 bunch celery, chopped
½ cup basil, chopped
1 tablespoon olive oil
Salt and pepper – to taste
Directions:
Heat olive oil in large pot over medium-high heat, add onion, with celery and cook until tender.
Pour chicken stock and tomatoes in the pot, bring mixture to simmer and season with salt and pepper. Simmer for 30 minutes.
Turn off heat and allow the soup to cool down. Puree in Nutri Bullet in batches.
Stir in heavy cream, basil, and Parmesan cheese.
Strain through a fine sieve or cheesecloth and serve immediately.
Nutrition:
Calories 140
Total Fat 7 g
Total Carbohydrate 17 g
Protein 3 g

Smoky soup V

Preparation Time: 15 minutes
Cooking Time: 40 minutes
Servings: 4
Ingredients:
3 red bell peppers, diced
1 ½ tablespoons grass-fed butter
2 carrots, grated
1 brown onion, diced
2 garlic cloves, minced
1 ½ tablespoon tomato puree
2 teaspoons fresh grated ginger
1 teaspoon smoked paprika
1 bay leaf
½ cup chilled coconut cream whisked with 1 tablespoon lemon juice
4 cups homemade vegetable stock
½ teaspoon ground coriander
Directions:
Melt butter in medium heavy-bottom pan, over medium-high heat.
Add carrots, bell peppers, and onion. Cook for 13-15 minutes or until onion is golden, stirring occasionally.
Add garlic, ginger, smoked paprika, tomato puree and coriander.
Cook until very fragrant, for 2 minutes.
Add bay leaf and stock; bring to boil and reduce heat to medium-low and simmer for 20-25 minutes.
Remove bay leaf and when cooled puree in batches using Nutribullet. Process until smooth.
Stir Strain in a fine sieve or cheesecloth and serve immediately.
Nutrition:
Calories 100
Total Fat 2 g
Total Carbohydrate 16 g
Protein 5 g

Onion and Peas Soup

Preparation Time: 10 minutes
Cooking Time: 25 minutes
Servings: 3
Ingredients
1 cup peas, boiled
2 carrots, peeled, chopped
1 onion, sliced
2 cups chicken broth
1 tablespoons lemon juice
4-5 garlic cloves, minced
½ teaspoon black pepper
¼ teaspoon salt
1 tablespoon oil
Directions
Heat oil in a saucepan, add onion and garlic cloves, fry for 2 minutes.
Add all peas and carrots stir for 5 minutes.
Add chicken broth, salt, pepper, and mix well.

Leave to cook on low heat for 15 minutes.
Strain and ladle into serving bowls.
Drizzle lemon juice.
Serve and enjoy.
Nutrition:
Calories 115
Total Fat 0 g
Total Carbohydrate 21 g
Protein 7 g

• Curried Carrot, Sweet Potato, and Ginger Soup V

Preparation Time: 10 minutes
Cooking Time: 35 minutes
Servings: 3
Ingredients:
Extra Virgin Olive Oil (2 tsp.)
Shallots (½ cup, chopped)
Sweet Potato (3 cups, peeled, cubed)
Carrots (1 ½ cup, peeled, sliced)
Directions:
Place a saucepan with your oil on medium heat until it just begins to smoke.
Add your shallots to the pot and sauté until it becomes tender (should take approximately 2 – 3 min).
Add all your prepped vegetables to the shallots, and your curry then allow to cook for another 2 minutes.
Pour in your broth and allow it to come to a boil. Once boiling, place the lid on the pot and reduce the heat to low.
Allow this mixture to simmer until your vegetables are all tender.
Once tender, add salt and pour your soup into a food processor. Pulse until creamy and smooth.
Strain, serve and Enjoy.
Tip: Consider topping with a teaspoon of vanilla Greek yogurt and sesame seeds.
Nutrition:
Calories 144
Total Fat 2.3 g
Total Carbohydrate 27.3 g
Protein 4.1 g

Breakfast

Lettuce power pack

Preparation time: 15 min
Cooking time: 15 min
Servings: 1
Ingredients: 1 egg, large
1 white of an egg, large
125 ml baby spinach leaves, small pieces
2 tbsp fat-free feta, crumbled
2 tomato, roam, small pieces
Pinch of salt, kosher or sea
Black pepper
1 large lettuce leaf, preferably not iceberg
Directions:
Place the first seven ingredients in a bowl and whisk well. Have a nonstick pan heating on medium heat, add the combined mixture, and cook to the consistency of your choice. Place the cooked ingredients on one end of the leaf and roll up.
Nutrition:
Calories 52
Total Fat 2.9g
Total Carbohydrate 5.6g
Protein 1.1g

Greek egg muffins

Preparation time: 5 min
Cooking time: 10 min
Servings: 6
Can be made ahead and enjoyed throughout the week for breakfast or lunch.
Ingredients: 5 eggs large
10 cherry tomatoes, quartered
5 artichoke hearts, marinated and diced
125 ml mozzarella cheese, low-fat and shredded
2 tbsp basil, fresh and minced
Pepper and salt for taste
Cooking time spray for the muffin tin
Directions:
While the oven is preheating to 350 degrees, break the eggs into a bowl and whisk well until smooth.
Combine the rest of the ingredients to the eggs and stir gently together.
Coat the muffin tin cups lightly with the cooking time spray.
Spoon the egg mixture into six cups, dividing it equally.
Bake for twenty min or 'til the eggs is set.
Let cool for a minute before savoring or store in the fridge to be enjoyed later.
Nutrition: Calories 106 Fats 6g Protein 10g

Sunday morning special

Preparation time: 20 min
Cooking time: 10 min
Servings: 1
Ingredients:
125 ml cottage cheese, low fat
1 egg, large
75 ml onion diced
1/4 tsp garlic minced
1 generous tbsp whole wheat flour
Pepper and salt for taste
Cooking time spray for the pan
Directions:
Spray the pan and pre-heat for a minute.
Sauté the garlic and onions, while stirring together the egg, cottage cheese, flour and pepper, and salt.
Add the cooked ingredients to the bowl mixture, stirring until well-combined.
Spray the pan again and spoon in the mixture to pan. Create 4 pancakes.
Cook on each side for four min.
Nutrition: Protein: 36 kcal Fat: 96 kcal
Carbohydrates: 10 kcal

Lemony Raspberries Bowls

Preparation time: 5 minutes
Cooking time: 12 minutes
Servings: 1
Ingredients

- 1 C. raspberries
- 2 tbsps. butter
- 2 tbsps. lemon juice

- 1 tsp. cinnamon powder

Directions
1. In your air fryer, mix all the ingredients, toss, and cover.
2. Cook at 350°F for 12 minutes.
3. Divide into bowls and serve for breakfast.

Nutrition
- Calories: 208 kcal.
- Fat: 6 g.
- Fiber: 9 g.
- Carbs: 14 g.
- Protein: 3 g.

Pancetta and Spinach Frittata

Preparation time: 15 minutes
Cooking time: 16 minutes
Servings: 1
Ingredients
- ¼ C. pancetta
- ½ tomato, cubed
- ¼ C. fresh baby spinach
- 3 eggs
- 1 tsp. salt and ground black pepper, as required
- ¼ C. Parmesan cheese, grated

Directions
1. Heat a nonstick skillet over medium heat and cook the pancetta for about 5 minutes.
2. Add the tomato and spinach cook for about 2–3 minutes.
4. Remove from the heat and drain the grease from the skillet.
5. Set aside to cool slightly.
6. Meanwhile, in a small bowl, add the eggs, salt, and black pepper and beat well.
7. In the bottom of a greased baking pan, place the pancetta mixture and top with the eggs, followed by the cheese.
8. Press the "Power Button" of the air fry oven and turn the dial to select the "Air Fry" mode.
9. Press the time button and again turn the dial to set the cooking time to 8 minutes.
10. Now push the temp button and rotate the dial to set the temperature at 355°F.
11. Press the "start/pause" button to start.
12. When the unit beeps to show that it is preheated, open the lid.
13. Arrange pan over the "wire rack" and insert in the oven.
14. Cut into equal-sized wedges and serve.

Nutrition
- Calories: 287 kcal.
- Total fat: 20.8 g.
- Saturated fat: 7.2 g.
- Cholesterol: 285 mg.
- Sodium: 915 mg.
- Total carbs: 1.7 g.
- Fiber: 0.3 g.
- Sugar: 0.9 g.

Protein: 23.1 g.

Chicken and Zucchini Omelet

Preparation time: 15 minutes
Cooking time: 35 minutes
Servings: 1
Ingredients

- 8 eggs
- ½ C. milk
- 1 tsp. salt and ground black pepper, as required
- 1 C. cooked chicken, chopped
- 1 C. Cheddar cheese, shredded
- ½ C. fresh chives, chopped
- ¾ C. zucchini, chopped

Directions

1. In a bowl, add the eggs, milk, salt, and black pepper and beat well. Add the remaining ingredients and stir to combine.
2. Place the mixture into a greased baking pan.
3. Press the "Power Button" of the Air Fry Oven and turn the dial to select the "Air Bake" mode.
4. Press the "Time" button and again turn the dial to set the cooking time to 35 minutes.
5. Now push the "Temp" button and rotate the dial to set the temperature at 315°F.
6. Press the "Start/Pause" button to start. When the unit beeps to show that it is preheated, open the lid.
7. Arrange pan over the wire rack and insert in the oven.
8. Cut into equal-sized wedges and serve hot.

Nutrition

- Calories: 209 kcal.
- Total fat: 13.3 g.
- Saturated fat: 6.3 g.
- Cholesterol: 258 mg.
- Sodium: 252 mg.
- Total carbs: 2.3 g.
- Fiber: 0.3 g
- Sugar: 1.8 g.
- Protein: 9.8 g.

Breakfast Pea Tortilla

Preparation time: 10 minutes
Cooking time: 7 minutes
Servings: 1
Ingredients

- ½ lb. baby peas
- 4 tbsps. butter
- 1 ½ C. yogurt
- 8 eggs
- ½ C. mint, chopped
- 1 tsp. salt and black pepper to the taste

Directions

1. Heat up a pan that fits your air fryer with the butter over medium heat, add peas, stir and cook for a couple of minutes.
2. Meanwhile, in a bowl, mix half of the yogurt with salt, pepper, eggs, and mint and whisk well.
3. Pour this over the peas, toss, introduce in your air fryer and cook at 350°F for 7 minutes.
4. Spread the rest of the yogurt over your tortilla, slice, and serve. Enjoy!

Nutrition

- Calories: 192 kcal.
- Fat: 5 g.
- Fiber: 4 g.
- Carbs: 8 g.
- Protein: 7 g.

Mushroom Cheese Salad

Preparation time: 10 minutes
Cooking time: 15 minutes
Servings: 1
Ingredients

- 10 mushrooms, halved
- 1 tbsp. fresh parsley, chopped
- 1 tbsp. olive oil

- 1 tbsp. Mozzarella cheese, grated
- 1 tbsp. Cheddar cheese, grated
- 1 tbsp. dried mix herbs
- 1 tsp. pepper
- 1 tsp. salt

Directions

1. Add all ingredients into the bowl and toss well.
2. Transfer bowl mixture into the air fryer baking dish.
3. Place in the air fryer and cook at 380°F for 15 minutes.
4. Serve and enjoy.

Nutrition

- Calories: 90 kcal.
- Fat: 7 g.
- Carbohydrates: 2 g.
- Sugar: 1 g.
- Protein: 5 g.
- Cholesterol: 7 mg.

Blueberry Chia Overnight Oats

Preparation time: 10 minutes
Cooking time: 30 minutes
Servings: 3
Ingredients

- 2 tbsp. chia seeds
- ¼ C. rolled oats
- 1 C. unsweetened vanilla almond milk
- ½ C. blueberries
- ½ tbsp. honey, maple syrup, agave, or 1 packet of Stevia

Directions

1. Combine all of the ingredients.
2. Refrigerate for 4 hours before serving.
3. The blueberries can be added to the overnight oats before or after mixing.
4. Add them just before serving if you're going to have them in the fridge for a couple of nights.

Nutrition

- Calories: 309 kcal.
- Protein: 9 g.
- Total carbs: 43 g.
- Dietary fiber: 12 g.
- Total fat: 12g.

Carrot Oatmeal

Preparation time: 10 minutes
Cooking time: 20 minutes
Servings: 3
Ingredients

- ½ C. shredded carrot, about 1 medium carrot
- ½ tsp. cinnamon
- 1 tsp. dash of nutmeg
- 1 C. quick oats, old fashioned oats work too
- ⅓ C. raisins
- 1 tbsp. maple syrup
- Optional: Pecans or walnuts for topping

Directions

1. Heat a saucepan over medium-high heat.
2. Cook for 1 minute after adding the shredded carrots.
3. In a saucepan, add ¾ C. of water, cinnamon, and nutmeg.
4. Get the water to a boil.
5. Add the oats.
6. Cook for 60–90 seconds.
7. Turn the burner off.
8. Add the raisins and maple syrup.
9. Cover and set aside for 2–3 minutes.
10. Divide into two dishes, top with nuts if desired, and serve!

Nutrition

- Calories: 261 kcal.
- Protein: 6 g.
- Total carbs: 59 g.
- Dietary fiber: 6 g.
- Total fat: 3 g.

Pumpkin Pie Bliss Protein Shake

Preparation time: 10 minutes
Cooking time: 30 minutes
Servings: 3
Ingredients

- 8 oz. non-fat milk
- 1 tbsp. protein powder base
- 2 tbsp. chai protein powder
- 2 tbsps. half and half
- 1 tbsp. sugar-free vanilla syrup
- 1 ½ tbsps. 100% pumpkin puree, not pumpkin pie filling

Directions

1. Combine all ingredients in a shaker and gently stir to properly combine.
2. Pour over ice with a dollop of whipped cream and a pinch of cinnamon or pumpkin pie spice on top.
3. For a frozen protein drink, mix all ingredients in a blender with 4–5 ice cubes and process until thick and smooth.

Nutrition

- Calories: 194 kcal.
- Protein: 29 g.
- Total carbs: 9 g.
- Dietary fiber: 5 g.
- Total fat: 3 g.

Apricot Overnight Oatmeal Recipe

Preparation time: 10 minutes
Cooking time: 30 minutes
Servings: 3
Ingredients

- ½ C. old fashion oats
- 1 tsp. ground cinnamon
- ¼ tsp. ground allspice
- ¼ tsp. ground ginger
- 1 tsp. pure vanilla extract
- ¼ C. dried, chopped apricots, no sugar added

Directions

For overnight oats:

1. Toss all of the ingredients in a small zip-top baggie and freeze for up to 6 months.
2. Place your oats in a container or covered bowl with 1 C. of milk (any kind) the night before you plan to eat them and leave them in the fridge overnight.
3. Warm on the stovetop or in the microwave if desired.

For cooking oats:

1. Toss all of the ingredients in a small zipper-top baggie and freeze for a possible busy morning.
2. When you're ready to prepare, add the bag's contents with 1 C. of milk (any kind) in a small pot and cook according to the oats box instructions.

Nutrition

- Calories: 266 kcal.
- Protein: 7 g.
- Total carbs: 54 g.
- Dietary fiber: 9 g.
- Total fat: 3g

Souffle Omelet With Mushrooms

Preparation time: 10 minutes
Cooking time: 20 minutes
Servings: 3
Ingredients

- 1 tsp. olive oil
- 1 clove garlic minced
- 8 oz. mushrooms sliced
- 1 tbsp. parsley minced
- 3 large eggs separated
- ¼ C. Cheddar cheese fat-free, shredded

Directions

1. Heat the olive oil in a skillet over medium heat and sauté the garlic. Sauté for 10 minutes with the mushrooms.
2. Remove the pan from the heat and add the parsley, and set aside.

3. Whisk the egg yolks until they are thickened. The whites can then be whisked until they are white and frothy. (The egg whites can be blended in a blender.)

4. Fold the whites into the yolks, season with salt and pepper, and fold in the cheese. Using a non-stick spray, coat a big skillet.

5. Cover and pour in the egg mixture.

6. Cook until the top and bottom of the layer is set. Carefully loosen it with the aid of a spatula.

7. Fold the omelet over carefully after adding the mushrooms.

8. Serve immediately.

Nutrition
- Calories: 329 kcal.
- Protein: 31 g.
- Total carbs: 10 g.
- Dietary fiber: 2 g.

Total fat: 20 g.

• Simple sunshine scramble

Preparation time: 5 min
Cooking time: 10 min
Servings: 1
Ingredients:
1 egg
1 clove garlic, small minced
1 tsp pesto
2 cherry tomatoes, quartered
1-piece bacon turkey, crumbled
1 tsp parmesan cheese, grated fine
Cooking time spray for the pan
Directions:
Lightly whisk the egg in a mixing bowl. Add a dash of water to the egg and the pesto. Whisk again lightly. Spray the pan lightly with cooking time spray and heat to medium-high.

Sauté the garlic until the aroma is released. Stir in bacon to crisp.

Slide pan contents out onto a side dish. Add tomatoes to the pan, sauté until liquid is almost gone. Add egg mixture to the pan and cook as for how you prefer your scrambled eggs. Stir in the bacon/garlic mixture and parmesan cheese just before the eggs are cooked.

Servings: with a slice of orange for that complete sunshine feel.

Nutrition:
Protein: 60 kcal Fat: 144 kcal
Carbohydrates: 8 kcal

• Black beans puree with scrambled eggs

Preparation time: 20 min
Cooking time: 30 min
Servings: 1
Ingredients:
For making the scrambled egg part of the recipe
1/8 teaspoon salt
1 egg
1/8 teaspoon pepper
Black beans puree
3 tablespoons enchilada sauce (green)
1/2 cup rinsed black beans
2 tablespoon vegetable or chicken broth
1 tablespoon protein powder
Directions:
Black beans puree:
Put the beans in some small sized saucepan on medium heat. Then put the enchilada sauce. Heat for 2 min. Keep stirring all the time. Then add the chicken broth.
Shift the mixture to one blender or use one hand blender to make a smooth mixture. Transfer it into one bowl.
Let it cool a bit and then mix the protein powder. Stir well. Cover it to keep it warm till you cook the egg.
Keep the leftovers in the fridge so that you can eat them at some other time.
Scrambled egg:
Heat one non-stick pan on medium heat. In the meantime, put the egg in one small bowl and whisk it well to incorporate air into it.
Pour the egg into the heated pan. Sprinkle pepper and salt. Use one rubber spatula for moving the egg in the pan while it is getting cooked. When it is almost done and still has a slightly liquid texture, you should fold it and take it out on a plate.
Put 1 tablespoon of the black beans puree. Also, put 1 teaspoon of enchilada sauce (green).
Note: it provides approximately 5 grams of fat, 11 grams of proteins, and 6 grams of carbohydrates.
Nutrition:
Calories 52
Total Fat 2.9g
Total Carbohydrate 5.6g
Protein 1.1g

• Veggie quiche muffins

Preparation time: 20 min
Cooking time: 30 min
Servings: 12
Ingredients:
¾ c. Shredded cheddar
1c. Green onion 1 c. Chopped broccoli
1 c. Diced tomatoes 2 c. Milk
4 eggs 1 pc. Pancake mix
1 tsp. Oregano ½ tsp. Salt tsp. Pepper
Directions:
Set oven to 375 degrees f, and lightly grease a 12-cup muffin tin with oil.
Sprinkle tomatoes, broccoli, onions and cheddar into muffin cups.
combine remaining ingredients in a medium bowl, whisk to combine then pour evenly on top of veggies.
Set to bake in preheated oven for about 40 min or until golden brown.
allow to cool slightly (about 5 min) then servings. Enjoy!
Nutrition: Calories: 58.8, fat: 3.2g, carbs: 2.9g, protein: 5.1g

• Steel cut oat blueberry pancakes

Preparation time: 10 min
Cooking time: 10 min
Servings: 4
Ingredients:
1½ c. Water
½ c. Oats 1/8 tsp. Salt
1 c. Flour ½ tsp. Baking powder
½ tsp. Baking soda 1 egg
1 c. Milk ½ c. Greek yogurt
1 c. Frozen blueberries ¾ c. Agave nectar
Directions:
Combine oats, salt, and water together in a medium saucepan, stir, and allow to come to a boil over high heat.
Set it to low and simmer for 10 min, or until oats are tender. Set aside.

Combine all remaining ingredients, except agave nectar, in a medium bowl, then fold in oats.
preheat griddle and lightly grease. Cook ¼ cup of batter at a time for about 3 min per side. Garnish with agave.
Nutrition: Calories: 257, fat: 7g, carbs: 46g, protein: 14g

• Very berry muesli

Preparation time: 2 hours
Cooking time: 4 hours
Servings: 2
Ingredients:
1 c. Oats
1 c. Fruit flavored yogurt
½ c. Milk
1/8 tsp. Salt
½ c. Dried raisins
½ c. Chopped apple
½ c. Frozen blueberries
¼ c. Chopped walnuts
Directions:
combine yogurt, salt and oats together in a medium bowl, mix well, then cover the mixture tightly.
Place in the refrigerator to cool for 6 hours.
add raisins, and apples the gently fold.
Top with walnuts and servings. Enjoy!
Nutrition: Calories: 198, carbs: 31.2g, fat: 4.3g, protein: 6g

• Strawberry & mushroom breakfast sandwich

Preparation time: 5 min
Cooking time: 5 min
Servings: 4
Ingredients:
8 oz. Cream cheese
1 tbsp. Honey
1 tbsp. Grated lemon zest
4 sliced portobello mushrooms
2 c. Sliced strawberries
Directions:
Add honey, lemon zest and cheese to a food processor, and process until fully incorporated.
.use cheese mixture to spread on mushrooms as you would butter.
Top with strawberries. Enjoy!
Nutrition:
Calories: 180, fat: 16g. Carbs: 6g, protein: 2g

• Shakshuka egg bake

Preparation time: 10 min
Cooking time: 30 min
Servings: 4
Ingredients:
1 teaspoon extra-virgin olive oil
½ onion, minced
1 garlic clove, minced
½ teaspoon smoked paprika
½ teaspoon ground cumin
1 (15-ounce) can diced tomatoes
2 ounces feta cheese, crumbled
4 large eggs
Directions:
Preheat the oven to 350°f.
In a medium skillet over medium heat, heat the oil. Add the onions and garlic, and sauté until translucent, about 5 min. Add the paprika and cumin, and cook a minute longer.
Stir in the tomatoes until well combined. Simmer until some of their liquid has evaporated and the mixture begins to thicken to form a sauce, 5 to 10 min.
Divide the sauce evenly among 4 ramekins, and repeat with the cheese, sprinkling evenly across.
Using a spoon, create wells in the tomato sauce and crack an egg over each, being careful to keep the yolk intact.
Bake in the ramekins for 15 min, until the yolk is done to your liking, longer if you like a hard-cooked yolk, and servings. (if you do not have ramekins, crack the eggs into spoon-made wells in the pan and let cook for 5 to 10 min, or per your preference.)
Post-op Servings: suggestions
Ingredient tip: for a variation on flavor, add diced bell pepper, chopped spinach, or chili powder.
Nutrition: calories: 144; total fat: 9g; protein: 9g; carbohydrates: 7g; fiber: 1g; sugar: 4g; sodium: 455mg.

Ricotta baked in the oven

Preparation time: 10 min
Cooking time: 30 min
Serving: 4
Ingredients:
1/4th cup parmesan cheese (grated)
1/2 cup ricotta cheese (low fat)
1 teaspoon Dijon mustard
1 teaspoon thyme (ground)
1/4th cup cheddar cheese (shredded)
1 egg
Directions:
Heat the oven to a temperature of 400f.
Put all the ingredients in one bowl. Stir and mix them well. The mixture will appear to be gritty and slightly brown. But it must be smooth.
Use one cookie scoop and divide the mixture into 4 wells of the muffin pan. You can use muffin pans made of silicone as you can use them easily and clean them quickly.
Bake it for about 20 min. Then remove from the oven and let it cool a bit. It is ready to be servings.
Note: this recipe is for making four ricotta muffins. Every muffin provides approximately 4 grams of fat, 4 grams of carbohydrates and 8 grams of proteins.

Poached eggs Italian style

Preparation time: 10 min
Cooking time: 10 min
Serving: 4
Ingredients:
3 to 4 pieces of jarred red pepper (roasted and sliced)
16 oz of marinara sauce (with the lowest level of sugar)
4 eggs 4 leaves of fresh basil
1 pinch of salt 1 pinch of pepper
Directions: Heat a big, rimmed skillet on medium heat. Put the marinara sauce. Then add the red peppers. Crack the eggs one by one making a "well" with the back of one spoon. Sprinkle pepper and salt.
Allow it to cook till the eggs become firm or for around 12 min. If you'd like you can put the lid for 2 min at the end.
Remove from the heat. Sprinkle basil and Servings: in a bowl or plate.

Note
Nutrition: 6 grams of fat, 8 grams of proteins, and 7 grams of carbohydrates.

Denver egg muffins with ham crust

Preparation time: 15 min
Cooking time: 30 min
Servings: 12
Ingredients
nonstick cooking time spray
12 slices deli ham ½ cup cheddar cheese
1 teaspoon extra-virgin olive oil
½ onion, diced ½ green pepper, minced
10 large eggs ¼ cup low-fat milk
Directions:
Preheat the oven to 350°f.
Grease a 12-compartment muffin tin with cooking time spray.
Line each cup with a ham slice, pushing down to fit tightly against the edge of the well.
In a small skillet over medium heat, heat the oil. Add the onion and green pepper, and sauté for 3 min, or until soft. Remove from the heat, and drain any liquid from the pan.
In a large bowl, whisk the eggs and milk. Add the cheese and cooked vegetables, and whisk again.
Ladle ¼ cup of the egg mixture into each cup. If there is any left over, divide evenly among the cups.
Bake for 20 to 25 min, or just until the eggs are firm and no longer runny, and servings.
Post-op Servings: suggestions
Ingredient tip: switch things up, and be creative with your vegetables, meat, and cheese. Try broccoli and cheddar, sundried tomato and feta, or sausage with pepper jack cheese. Garnish with hot sauce, salsa, avocado, herbs, or light sour cream.
Nutrition: calories: 99; total fat: 6g; protein: 8g; carbohydrates: 1g; fiber: 0g; sugar: 1g; sodium: 206mg

Cheesy slow cooker egg casserole

Preparation time: 15 min
Cooking time: 4 to 8 hours
Servings: 8

55

Ingredients:
1-pound fresh Italian chicken sausage
Nonstick cooking time spray
1 (30-ounce) bag frozen hash browns
1 medium red bell pepper, seeded and diced
½ medium onion, diced
1 (4-ounce) can mild diced green chiles
1½ cups low-fat shredded cheddar cheese, divided into three ½-cup servings:
12 large eggs 1 cup low-fat milk
½ teaspoon salt
½ teaspoon freshly ground black pepper
Directions:
Remove the casings from the sausage, and discard.
In a large skillet over medium heat, brown the meat, breaking into smaller pieces as it cooks, about 7 min, or until no longer pink.
Spray a 5-quart slow cooker with nonstick cooking time spray, and layer half of the frozen hash browns, cooked sausage, pepper, onion, and chiles, plus ½ cup of cheese. Repeat with the remaining hash browns, sausage, pepper, onion, and chiles, plus another ½ cup of cheese.
In a large bowl, whisk the eggs, milk, salt, and pepper.
Pour the egg mixture over the potato-sausage layers, and top with remaining ½ cup of cheese.
Cook on high for 4 hours or on low for 8 hours, and servings.
Post-op Servings: suggestions
Ingredient tip: if you cannot find fresh Italian chicken sausage, look for precooked sausage in the refrigerator section of your grocery store. Dice into small pieces and brown in a skillet before adding to the slow cooker.
Nutrition: calories: 348; total fat: 17g; protein: 27g; carbohydrates: 24g; fiber: 3g; sugar: 3g; sodium: 783mg.

• Make-ahead breakfast burritos

Preparation time: 15 min
Cooking time: 20 min
Servings: 8
Ingredients:
12 large eggs
¼ cup low-fat milk
1 teaspoon extra-virgin olive oil
½ medium yellow onion, diced
1 medium green bell pepper, seeded and diced
1 cup canned black beans, drained and rinsed
8 (7- to 8-inch) whole wheat tortillas
½ cup shredded cheddar cheese
8 ounces salsa
Directions
In a large bowl, whisk together the eggs and milk.
In a large skillet over medium heat, heat the oil. Add the onion, bell pepper, and black beans. Sauté until the onion is translucent, about 5 min, and transfer to a plate.
Pour the egg mixture into the skillet, and gently stir until the eggs are fluffy and firm. Remove from the heat.
Divide the eggs and onion mixture evenly among the tortillas, and top with the cheese and salsa.
With both sides of the first tortilla tucked in, roll tightly to close. Repeat with the remaining tortillas.
Servings: immediately, or freeze for up to 3 months. If freezing, wrap the burritos in paper towels, and cover tightly with aluminum foil for storage.
Post-op Servings: suggestions
Ingredient tip: if you cannot tolerate doughy textures after surgery, skip the tortilla and spoon the filling in a bowl.
Nutrition: calories: 264; total fat: 12g; protein: 21g; carbohydrates: 24g; fiber: 11g; sugar: 3g; sodium: 593mg.

• Baked broccoli and eggs

Preparation time: 10 min
Cooking time: 15 min
Servings: 1
Ingredients:
Margarine, light (4 ounces)
Broccoli, frozen, thawed, chopped (10 ounces)
Pimento, jarred, chopped (4 ounces)
Flour (6 tablespoons)
Black pepper, freshly ground (1 dash)
Mushrooms, sliced, fresh (1/2 cup)
Eggs, large (6 pieces)
Cheddar cheese, low fat (1/2 pound)
Cottage cheese, nonfat (2 pounds)
Salt (1 teaspoon)
Paprika (1 dash)
Directions:
Set the oven to 350 degrees to preheat.
Meanwhile, place the eggs, broccoli, and all other ingredients in a large bowl. Stir to combine.
Use cooking time spray to coat the sides and bottom of a casserole dish (2-quart).
Fill the preparation time dish with the broccoli-egg mixture, making sure to spread it evenly.
Bake in the oven for one hour and thirty min.
Servings: immediately.
Nutrition: Calories: 129kcal carbohydrates: 2g protein: 10g fat: 9g saturated fat: 4g cholesterol: 179mg sodium: 218mg potassium: 113mg fiber: 1g sugar: 2g vitamin a: 363iu vitamin c: 1mg calcium: 142mg iron: 1mg

• Black bean and pumpkin soup

Preparation time: 5 min
Cooking time: 15 min
Servings: 2 cups
Ingredients:
Onion, medium, chopped (1 piece)
Black pepper, freshly ground (1/2 teaspoon)
Pumpkin puree, canned (16 ounces)
Cumin, ground (1 tablespoon)
Tomatoes, canned, diced (1 cup)
Olive oil, extra virgin (2 tablespoons)
Garlic cloves, minced (4 pieces)
Chili powder (1 teaspoon)
Black beans, canned, rinsed, drained (30 ounces)
Beef broth, low sodium (2 cups)
Directions:
Heat a soup kettle on medium after filling with the oil.
Add the garlic, onions, pepper, chili powder, and cumin. Stir and cook for about two to three min or until soft and fragrant.
Add the broth as well as pumpkin, tomatoes, and black beans. Stir to combine.
Allow the mixture to simmer, uncovered, for twenty-five min or until thickened to your desired consistency.
Remove from heat and process the black bean and pumpkin soup with an immersion blender.
Servings: and enjoy.
Nutrition:
Calories: 266kcal carbohydrates: 13g
protein: 4g fat: 24g saturated fat: 21g
sodium: 879mg potassium: 641mg
fiber: 3g sugar: 4g vitamin a: 17726iu
vitamin c: 23mg calcium: 71mg
iron: 6mg

• Broccoli and tofu quiche

Preparation time: 10 min
Cooking time: 15 min
Servings: 3
Ingredients:
Salt (1/4 teaspoon)
Mushrooms, chopped (1/4 pound)
Pickled plum/ white miso paste (1 tablespoon)
Yellow onion, chopped (1 piece)
Sesame tahini (2 tablespoons)
Bulgur wheat, uncooked (1/2 cup)
Sesame oil (1 tablespoon)
Broccoli, chopped (1/2 pound)
Tofu (1 ½ pounds)
Tamari (1tablespoon) directions:
Set the oven at 350 degrees to preheat.
Directions:
Fill a small pot with water (1 cup) and heat on medium. Bring to a boil before adding in the bulgur and salt. Stir to combine and allow the mixture to boil again. Reduce heat to low and cover to cook for about—

fifteen min. Meanwhile, grease a pie pan (9-inch) with a little oil. Pour the cooked bulgur into the pie pan, pressing lightly to spread it evenly at the bottom. Place in the oven to bake for about twelve min or until crusty on top. Let stand to cool. Heat a large skillet (nonstick) on medium-high before adding the onions. Stir in the mushrooms and broccoli and cook for two min. Cover and immediately remove from heat. Meanwhile, fill the food processor with the tofu. Add the tamari, tahini, and umeboshi paste. Process until well-combined and smooth, then pour into a large bowl. Add the cooked veggies and gently toss until evenly coated. Transfer the veggie mixture onto the crusted bulgur. Bake in the oven for about half an hour. Once done, let stand on a wire rack. After ten min, slice into 6 portions and Servings: immediately.

Nutrition: Calories: 248kcal carbohydrates: 27.2g protein: 30.6g fat: 3.6g saturated fat: 0.4g cholesterol: 50mg sodium: 718mg fiber: 6.1g

Cheese-filled acorn squash

Preparation time: 10 min
Cooking time: 50 min
Servings: 3
Ingredients:
Tofu, firm (1 pound)
Basil (1 teaspoon)
Black pepper, freshly ground (1 pinch)
Onion, chopped finely (1 teaspoon)
Garlic powder (1 teaspoon)
Cheddar cheese, reduced fat, shredded (1 cup)
Acorn squash, halved, seeded (2 pieces)
Celery, diced (1 cup)
Mushrooms, fresh, sliced (1 cup)
Oregano (1 teaspoon)
Salt (1/8 teaspoon)
Tomato sauce (8 ounces)
Directions:
Set the oven at 350 degrees to preheat.
Arrange the acorn squash pieces, with their cut-sides facing down, at the bottom of a glass dish.
Place in the microwave oven and cook for about twenty min or until softened. Set aside.

Heat a saucepan (nonstick) on medium, then add the tofu (sliced into cubes). Cook until browned before stirring in the onion and celery. Cook for two min or until the onion is translucent.

Add the mushrooms. Stir to combine and cook for an additional two to three min. Pour in the tomato sauce as well as the dry seasonings.

Give everything a good stir, then spoon equal portions of the mixture inside the acorn squash pieces.

Cover and place in the oven to cook for about fifteen min. Uncover and top with the cheese before returning to the oven. Cook for five more min or until the cheese is melted and bubbling.

Servings: immediately.
Nutrition:
Calories: 328kcal
carbohydrates: 47.5g
protein: 16.9g
fat: 10.8g
saturated fat: 5.8g
polyunsaturated fat: 5g
cholesterol: 42mg
sodium: 557mg
fiber: 7.7g sugar: 5.9g

• Cheesy spinach bake

Preparation time: 5 min
Cooking time: 35 min
Servings: 4
Ingredients:
Eggs, whole (2 pieces)
Parmesan cheese (1/2 cup)
Cottage cheese, fat-free/ low fat (2 cups)
Spinach, frozen, thawed, drained (10 ounces)
Directions:
Set the oven to 350 degrees to preheat. Meanwhile, line a baking pan (8x8) with parchment paper.
Place all ingredients in a large bowl. Stir to combine. Pour the cheesy spinach mixture into the preparation time bed pan. Place in the oven to bake for twenty to thirty min or until the cheese on top is bubbling.
Remove from the oven and allow to cool for five min.
Servings: sprinkled with garlic, salt, and pepper.
Enjoy.
Nutrition:
Servings: 1g calories: 292kcal carbohydrates: 4.5g protein: 26g fat: 19.1g saturated fat: 7.2g monounsaturated fat: 11.9g cholesterol: 545mg sodium: 735mg fiber: 2g

• Southwestern Scrambled Egg Burritos

Prep Time: 10 Minutes
Cook Time: 10 Minutes
Total Time: 20 Minutes
Servings: 8
Ingredients:
12 eggs
¼ cup low-fat milk
1 teaspoon extra-virgin olive oil
½ onion, chopped
1 red bell pepper, diced
1 green bell pepper, diced
1 (15-ounce) can black beans, drained and rinsed
8 (7- to 8-inch) whole-wheat tortillas, such as La Tortilla Factory low-carb tortillas
1 cup salsa, for serving
Directions:
Using a big bowl stir the eggs and milk. Set aside.
In a large skillet over medium-high heat, heat the olive oil and add the onion and bell peppers. Sauté for 2 to 3 minutes, or until tender. Add the beans and stir to combine.
Add the egg mixture. Minimize heat and mix while constantly with a rubber spatula for 5 minutes, until the eggs are fluffy and cooked through.
Divide the scrambled egg mixture among the tortillas. Fold over the bottom end of the tortilla, fold in the sides, and roll tightly to close.
Serve immediately with the salsa, or place each burrito in a zip-top bag and refrigerate for up to 1 week. To eat, reheat each burrito in the microwave for 60 to 90 seconds. These will also keep well in the freezer for up to 1 month.
Serving tip: To get more vegetables into your breakfast, buy a bag of frozen California-blend mixed vegetables. Heat some in a skillet with extra-virgin olive oil, add eggs, and—voilà!—a quick veggie-packed egg burrito.
Nutrition:
Per Serving (1 burrito): Calories: 250; Total fat: 10g; Protein: 19g; Carbs: 28g; Fiber: 13g; Sugar: 1g; Sodium: 546mg

• Smoothie Bowl With Greek Yogurt And Fresh Berries

Prep Time: 5 MINUTES
Cook Time: 5 MINUTES
Total Time: 10 MINUTES
Servings: 1
Ingredients
¾ cup unsweetened vanilla almond milk or low-fat milk
¼ cup low-fat plain Greek yogurt
1/3 cup (1 handful) fresh spinach
½ scoop (1/8 cup) plain or vanilla protein powder
¼ cup frozen mixed berries
¼ cup fresh raspberries
¼ cup fresh blueberries
1 tablespoon sliced, slivered almonds
1 teaspoon chia seeds
Directions:

In a blender, combine the milk, yogurt, spinach, protein powder, and frozen berries. For 4 minutes blend, until the powder is well dissolved and no longer visible.

Pour the smoothie into small bowl.

Decorate the smoothie with the fresh raspberries, blueberries, almonds, and chia seeds.

Serve with a spoon and enjoy!

Serving tip: You can make this smoothie bowl with a variety of other fruits and toppings to change it up. Try a mango-pineapple version. Top with unsweetened, flaked coconut and use coconut milk in the smoothie base for a more tropical vibe.

Nutrition:

Per Serving (1 bowl): Calories: 255; Total fat: 10 g; Protein: 20g; Carbs: 21g; Fiber: 8g; Sugar: 10g; Sodium: 262mg

Cherry-Vanilla Baked Oatmeal

Prep Time: 10 MINUTES
Cook Time: 45 MINUTES
Total Time: 55 MINUTES
Servings: 6

Ingredients

Nonstick cooking spray
1 cup old-fashioned oats
½ teaspoon ground cinnamon
¾ teaspoon baking powder
1 tablespoon ground flaxseed
3 eggs
1 cup low-fat milk
½ cup low-fat plain Greek yogurt
1 teaspoon vanilla extract
1 teaspoon liquid stevia (optional; to improve sweetness)
1 cup fresh pitted cherries
1 apple, peeled, cored and chopped

Directions:

Preheat the oven to 375°F. Lightly coat an 8-by-8-inch baking dish with the cooking spray.

Mix together the oats, cinnamon, baking powder, and flaxseed in a medium bowl. In a separate large bowl, gently whisk the eggs, milk, yogurt, vanilla, and stevia (if using).

Combine the dry ingredients and mix to combine. Gently fold in the cherries and apples.

Bake for 45 minutes or until the edges start to pull away from the side of the pan and the oatmeal gently bounces back when touched.

Divide leftover oatmeal into airtight glass containers. Refrigerate for up to 1 week for quick and easy breakfast, or freeze.

Serving tip: Experiment with the fixings in your baked oatmeal. I like to make my recipes seasonal. Replace the yogurt with pumpkin puree to add a hint of fall. Try using unsweetened dried cranberries instead of cherries for a holiday twist. Swap out apples and cherries for 2 cups fresh berries in spring for a very berry oatmeal! For the creamiest consistency, I recommend topping with a ¼ cup low-fat milk at serving time.

Nutrition:

Per Serving (½ cup): Calories: 149; Total fat: 4g; Protein: 8g; Carbs: 21g; Fiber: 4g; Sugar: 9g; Sodium: 71 mg

High-Protein Pancakes

PREP TIME: 5 MINUTES
COOK TIME: 15 MINUTES
SERVINGS: 4

INGREDIENTS

3 eggs
1 cup low-fat cottage cheese
1/3 cup whole-wheat pastry flour
1½ tablespoons coconut oil, melted
Nonstick cooking spray

Directions:

In large bowl, lightly whisk the eggs.

Whisk in the cottage cheese, flour, and coconut oil just until combined.

Heat a large skillet or griddle over medium heat, and lightly coat with the cooking spray.

Using a measuring cup, pour 1/3 cup of batter into the skillet for each pancake, Boil for 3 minutes and till bubbles appear across the surface of each pancake

Flip over the pancakes and cook for 1 to 2 minutes on the other side, or until golden brown.

Serve immediately.

Serving tip: Top these pancakes with fresh berries and plain yogurt, unsweetened applesauce, or sugar-free syrup. You can even try them with natural peanut butter and bananas on a general diet.

Nutrition:

Per Serving (1 pancake): Calories: 182; Total fat: 10g; Protein: 12g; Carbs: 10g; Fiber: 3g; Sugar: 1g; Sodium: 68mg

Pumpkin Muffins With Walnuts And Zucchini

PREP TIME: 10 MINUTES
COOK TIME: 35 MINUTES
SERVINGS: 4

INGREDIENTS

Nonstick cooking spray or baking liners
2 cups old-fashioned oats
1¾ cups whole-wheat pastry flour
¼ cup ground flaxseed
2 tablespoons baking powder
1 teaspoon baking soda
1 teaspoon ground cinnamon
¼ teaspoon ground nutmeg
¼ teaspoon ground ginger
¼ teaspoon ground allspice
2 cups shredded zucchini
1 cup canned pumpkin or fresh pumpkin puree
1 cup low-fat milk
4 eggs, lightly beaten
¼ cup unsweetened applesauce
1 teaspoon liquid stevia
½ cup chopped walnuts

Directions:

Preheat the oven to 375°F. Prepare two muffin tins by coating the cups with the cooking spray, or use baking liners.

In large bowl, mix together the oats, flour, flaxseed, baking powder, baking soda, cinnamon, nutmeg, ginger, and allspice.

In a separate medium bowl mix together the zucchini, pumpkin, milk, eggs, applesauce, and stevia

Add the wet ingredients to the dry and stir to combine. Gently stir in the walnuts.

Fill the cups of the muffin tins about half full with the batter.

Bake until the muffins are done, when a toothpick inserted in the center comes out clean, about 25 minutes.

Let the muffins cool for 5 minutes before removing them from the tins. Place on a baking rack to finish cooling.

Wrap leftover muffins in plastic wrap and freeze. Reheat frozen muffins in the microwave for about 20 seconds.

Nutrition:

Per Serving (1 muffin): Calories: 128; Total fat: 5g; Protein: 5g; Carbs: 18g; Fiber: 3g; Sugar: 1g; Sodium: 86mg

• Hard-Boiled Eggs And Avocado On Toast

PREP TIME: 10 MINUTES
COOK TIME: 20 MINUTES
SERVINGS: 4

INGREDIENTS

4 eggs

4 slices sprouted whole-wheat bread, such as Angelic Bake house Sprouted Grain
1 medium avocado
1 teaspoon hot sauce
Freshly ground black pepper
Directions:
Using a pot fill it up and rapid boil over high heat.
Carefully add the eggs to the boiling water using a spoon, and set a timer for 10 minutes.
Immediately transfer the eggs from the boiling water to a strainer, and run cold water over the eggs to stop the cooking process.
Once the eggs are cool enough to handle, peel them and slice lengthwise into fourths.
Toast the bread.
While the bread toasts, mash the avocado with a fork in a small bowl and mix in the hot sauce.
Spread the avocado mash evenly across each toast. Top each toast slice with 4 egg slices and season with the black pepper.
Nutrition:
Per Serving (1 toast): Calories: 191; Total fat: 10g; Protein: 10g; Carbs: 15g; Fiber: 5g; Sugar: 1g; Sodium: 214mg

• Yogurt- Based Breakfast Popsicles

Prep Time: 5 Minutes
Cook Time: 4 hours
Servings: 6
Ingredients
½ cup regular or instant oats
1 cup Greek yogurt, plain, non-fat
1 cup mixed berries
½ cup milk 1% or skim
Directions:
Combine the yogurt and milk.
Distribute the milk and yogurt mixture in the Popsicle molds.
Add a few berries in all the molds.
Distribute the ½ cup oatmeal, evenly among each mound.
Leave the popsicles in the freezer for about 5 hours before serving.
If the popsicles don't come off easily, keep the mound under a little warm water until they come off loose.
Nutrition:
Calories 52
Total Fat 2.9g
Total Carbohydrate 5.6g
Protein 1.1g

• Shrimp Ceviche

Preparation Time: 10 minutes
Cooking Time: 25 minutes
Servings: 4
Ingredients:
4 Roma or Italian medium tomatoes, diced or 8 ounces canned tomatoes, diced.
1 small red onion, peeled and finely diced or approximately ¾ cup chopped red onion
1 bunch of fresh cilantro, stemmed and finely chopped
1 pound shrimp medium raw
1 cup lime juice or approximately 5 fresh limes, halved
2 serrano chili peppers with ribs, seeds removed and minced, if needed.
Directions:
In a large bowl, add the shrimp and lime juice.
Cover and let it marinate for 10 to 15 minutes at least or wait until the mixture changes to pink. Do not allow it to marinate for too long or the shrimp will "overcook" and get toughed or rubbery.
Combine the onions, tomatoes, cilantro and chili peppers.
Slowly stir to combine.
Season with salt as required.
Serve it when cold.
Nutrition:
Calories 52
Total Fat 2.9g
Total Carbohydrate 5.6g
Protein 1.1g

Chicken Caprese

Preparation Time: 15 mins
Cooking Time: 35 minutes
Servings: 4

Ingredients

4 thick slices ripe tomato (½-inch)
3 tablespoon balsamic vinegar
1 pound chicken breasts, boneless and skinless
4 1-ounce slices mozzarella cheese
1 tablespoon olive oil
1 teaspoon dry Italian seasoning or a mixture of garlic powder, dried basil and dried oregano.
2 tablespoon thinly sliced fresh basil
Pepper to season

Directions:

Apply 1 tablespoon of olive oil over the chicken breasts and season as required with salt and pepper.
2. Marinade the chicken with the Italian season and set it aside for 15 minutes.
3. Warm up a skillet or grill over medium to high heat.
4. Keep the chicken on the grill pan and let it cook for about 4-5 minutes on each side, or until it's as cooked as preferred. The cook time alters depending on how thick the chicken breasts are.
5. When the chicken is done, top it with a slice of mozzarella cheese and allow it to cook for another minute.
6. Take it off the heat and keep the chicken breasts on a plate.
7. Garnish the cooked chicken breast with a slice of tomato, evenly sliced basil and season with pepper to taste.
8. Sprinkle with balsamic vinegar or balsamic glaze before serving.

Nutrition:
Per Serving (½ cup): Calories: 149; Total fat: 4g; Protein: 8g; Carbs: 21g; Fiber: 4g; Sugar: 9g; Sodium: 71 mg

Black Bean and Corn Salad

Preparation Time: 15 mins
Cooking Time: 35 minutes
Servings: 6

Ingredients

2 tablespoon red onion, minced
¼ cup balsamic vinegar
1 teaspoon lemon juice
2 tablespoon olive oil
1 cup corn with the whole kernel
2 cans of black beans, rinsed and drained (16 ounces can)
¼ cup fresh parsley, chopped
1 teaspoon garlic, minced
1 teaspoon honey
salt and pepper for seasoning

Directions:

1. Combine the fresh corn, red onion, black beans, and fresh parsley in a medium-sized mixing bowl.
2. Transfer the balsamic vinegar, olive oil, lemon juice, honey, garlic, salt and, pepper.
3. Add this mixture to the black beans and corn mixture.
4. Allow the salad to marinate for half an hour before serving.

Italian Poached Eggs

Ingredients

16 oz. marinara sauce
4 shredded basil leaves
3-4 roasted red pepper, sliced
Pepper
4 eggs
Salt

Instructions

Grab a skillet and let it heat up. Add the marinara sauce and the peppers then mix them together and allow them to heat up.

Once they are hot, use a spoon to make four wells into the marinara sauce. Now, crack one egg into each of the wells you have made.

Sprinkle pepper and salt over each of the eggs.

Allow this to cook for about 12 minutes. You can cook the eggs as long as you want until it reaches your desired doneness. You can also place a lid on your skillet so that the eggs cook a bit faster.

Remove the skillet from the stove and sprinkle the torn basil over the top. Scoop the eggs out along with a bit of sauce and enjoy.

Nutrition:
Per Serving (½ cup): Calories: 149; Total fat: 4g; Protein: 8g; Carbs: 21g; Fiber: 4g; Sugar: 9g; Sodium: 71 mg

Soft Eggs with Chives and Ricotta

Preparation Time: 10 minutes
Cooking Time: 30 minutes
Servings: 4
Ingredients
2 eggs
Olive oil
½ c milk
1 tbsp. chopped chives
½ c ricotta

Directions:
Add the eggs and milk to a jar. Place the lid on tightly and shake it until everything is mixed together well.
Grab yourself a skillet and place it on the stove. Once it is warm, pour the eggs into the skillet and scramble them. Allow them to cook until they are soft-set. Once soft-set, let it cook and gently stir them once in a while.
After the eggs are done, stir the ricotta and the chives. Add the eggs to a plate and drizzle some oil over the top if you would like.
Nutrition:
Per Serving (½ cup): Calories: 149; Total fat: 4g; Protein: 8g; Carbs: 21g; Fiber: 4g; Sugar: 9g; Sodium: 71 mg

• Mocha Frappuccino

Preparation Time: 10 minutes
Cooking Time: 20 minutes
Servings: 4
Ingredients
¼ c brewed coffee
Low-sugar chocolate syrup
¼ c unsweetened almond milk
Low-fat whipped cream
½ c 0% fat Greek yogurt
1 c ice
3-4 drops liquid sweetener
1 tbsp. cocoa powder

Directions:
Place the coffee, ice, milk, cocoa, yogurt, and sweetener in a blender and pulse until all of the ingredients come together and it's all smooth.
Pour the Frappuccino into a glass and swirl some whipped cream and chocolate syrup over the top.
Nutrition:
Per Serving (½ cup): Calories: 149; Total fat: 4g; Protein: 8g; Carbs: 21g; Fiber: 4g; Sugar: 9g; Sodium: 71 mg

• Oatmeal Cookie Shake

Preparation Time: 10 minutes
Cooking Tim: 15 minutes
Servings: 3
Ingredients
Low-fat cream, cinnamon, and nuts – garnish
1 c low-fat nut milk
Ice
½ tsp. cinnamon
¼ tsp. vanilla
1 scoop vanilla whey protein powder
1 tbsp. oatmeal
Directions:
Place the protein powder, mice, milk, vanilla, cinnamon, and oatmeal into a strong blender, and pulse couple of times until all of the ingredients come together.
Pour the shake into a glass and top with some cinnamon, cream, and nuts.

Bun less Breakfast Sandwich

Ingredients
¼ c shredded cheddar cheese
2 eggs
2 tbsp. water
½ avocado, mashed
2 sliced cooked bacon

Instructions
Place two canning jar lids into a skillet and spray with cooking spray. Let everything warm up. Crack one egg in each lid and whisk the egg gently with a fork to break the yolks.

Pour a small amount of water into the pan and put the lid on the skillet. Allow to cook and steam the eggs. Cook for three minutes. Take off the lid and put cheese on just one of the eggs. Allow cheese to melt for about one minute.

Put the egg without the cheese on a plate. Add avocado and then the bacon on top. Put the other egg on top with the cheesy side down. Enjoy.

Ham and Egg Roll-Ups

Ingredients
2 tsp. garlic powder
1 c baby spinach
1 c chopped tomatoes
10 eggs
Pepper
2 tbsp. butter
Salt
1 ½ c shredded cheddar cheese
20 ham slices

Instructions
Turn oven to broil. Crack all the eggs into a bowl and beat together. Add the garlic powder, pepper, and salt. Mix well.

Warm a skillet on stove top. Add the butter and allow it to melt. Add the eggs and scramble until they are done. Mix the cheese, stirring until it melts. Fold in the spinach and tomatoes.

Put two pieces of ham on a cutting board. Add a spoonful of eggs then roll up. Repeat this process until all ham and eggs are used.

Place the roll-ups on a baking sheet and broil about five minutes.

Nutrition:
Per Serving (½ cup): Calories: 149; Total fat: 4g; Protein: 8g; Carbs: 21g; Fiber: 4g; Sugar: 9g; Sodium: 71 mg

Chocolate Porridge

Preparation Time: 10 minutes
Cooking Time: 30 minutes
Servings: 4

Ingredients
Chopped nuts, fruits, or seeds of choice
4 tbsp. porridge oats
1 c skim milk
Sugar-free syrup
1 square dark unsweetened chocolate
1 tbsp. cocoa powder

Directions:
Place the chocolate, cocoa powder, oats, and milk in a microwavable bowl.

Cook for two minutes. Give everything a good stir and cook for an additional 15 to 20 seconds.

Put in a serving bowl and add desired toppings. Enjoy.

Nutrition:
Per Serving (½ cup): Calories: 149; Total fat: 4g; Protein: 8g; Carbs: 21g; Fiber: 4g; Sugar: 9g; Sodium: 71 mg

Flour-Less Pancakes

Preparation Time: 15 minutes
Cooking Time: 20 minutes
Servings: 2

Ingredients
Milk to mix
1 egg
Low-fat cooking spray
1 c rolled oats
1 banana

Directions:
Place the banana, egg, and oats into a food processor. Process until smooth. Add a small amount of milk and blend again. Add the milk until the mixture has reached a runny consistency. Three tablespoons should be the maximum amount you use.

Allow to sit for about 15 minutes. This lets the mixture thicken slightly.

Spray a small amount of cooking spray into a skillet. Allow to get warm. Add a spoonful of the batter to form a small pancake. Put as many as your pan will allow. Just make sure you have room to flip each. Allow the first side to cook for about a minute until bubbles begin to form on the surface. Flip and cook until browned. Remove from the skillet onto a plate and keep warm while you continue to cook the remaining batter.

Serve warm with fruit, yogurt, sugar-free syrup, a dusting of powdered sugar, or a drizzle of lemon. You might prefer them plain. Either way, enjoy.

Nutrition:

Per Serving (½ cup): Calories: 149; Total fat: 4g; Protein: 8g; Carbs: 21g; Fiber: 4g; Sugar: 9g; Sodium: 71 mg

• Cheesy Spiced Pancakes

Preparation Time: 15 minutes
Cooking Time: 20 minutes
Servings: 3
Ingredients
Pancakes:
1 tbsp. artificial sweetener
1 tsp. mixed spice, ground
Low-fat cooking spray
8 oz. spreadable goat cheese
Pinch salt
3 eggs, separated
½ c all-purpose flour
Optional Adult Toppings:
Sweetener
1 measure Brandy
4 tangerines, peeled
2 oz. cranberries
Directions:
To make the pancakes: Combine the egg yolks, cheese, and mixed spice. Add the salt and flour and mix well.
Beat the egg whites until they are stiff peaks and whisk in sweetener. Fold this into the cheese mixture.
If using the optional topping, place sweetener and tangerines into a pot. Stir occasionally until tangerines begin to release some juices and begin to look a bit syrupy. Add the Brandy and cranberries. Let this cook for few minutes. Keep warm until ready to use.

Spray the skillet with cooking spray. Allow to warm up. Add three large spoonful of batter into the pan. Cook for about two minutes until bubbles form on top. Flip and cook until the other side is browned. Remove from the pan and keep warm. Continue until all batter has been used. You should get 12 pancakes from this batter.

Divide among four plates and spoon the topping. Enjoy.

Nutrition:

Per Serving (½ cup): Calories: 149; Total fat: 4g; Protein: 8g; Carbs: 21g; Fiber: 4g; Sugar: 9g; Sodium: 71 mg

• Egg Muffin

Preparation Time: 10 minutes
Cooking Time: 20 minutes
Servings: 4
Ingredients
¼ tsp. salt
12 slices turkey bacon
¼ tsp. Italian seasoning
6 large eggs
¼ tsp. pepper
¾ c shredded low-fat shredded cheese of choice
½ c 1% milk
Directions:
Spray cooking spray into muffin pan. Your oven needs to be warmed to 350.

Place three slices of bacon on the bottom of each muffin cup.

Mix all remaining ingredients together until well combined. Reserve ¼ cup of shredded cheese. Put a fourth cup of this mixture into every muffin cup. Add a bit more cheese on top.

Bake for about 25 minutes. The eggs should be set.

Nutrition:

Per Serving (½ cup): Calories: 149; Total fat: 4g; Protein: 8g; Carbs: 21g; Fiber: 4g; Sugar: 9g; Sodium: 71 mg

Cottage Cheese Pancakes

Preparation Time: 10 minutes
Cooking Time: 15 minutes
Servings: 4
Ingredients
1/3 c all-purpose flour
½ tbsp. canola oil
½ tsp. baking soda
3 eggs, lightly beaten
1 c low-fat cottage cheese
Directions:
Sift the baking soda and flour in a small bowl.
Mix the remaining ingredients together.
Mix the flour into the wet ingredients and stir to incorporate.
Spray cooking spray into a skillet and warm. When warmed, place one-third cup of the batter into the pan and cook until you see bubbles. Flip and cook until the other side is browned.
Serve warm with sugar-free syrup. Enjoy.
Nutrition:
Per Serving (½ cup): Calories: 149; Total fat: 4g; Protein: 8g; Carbs: 21g; Fiber: 4g; Sugar: 9g; Sodium: 71 mg

Lunch

Sheet Pan Zucchini Parmesan

Preparation Time: 10 minutes
Cooking Time: 25 Minutes
Servings: 6
Ingredients:
1 - cup panko
1/3 - cup freshly grated parmesan cheese
Kosher salt and freshly ground black pepper, to taste
2 - zucchinis, thinly sliced to 1/4-inch thick rounds
1/3 - cup all-purpose flour
2 - large eggs, beaten
½ - cup marinara sauce
½ - cup mozzarella pearls, drained
2 - tablespoons chopped fresh parsley leaves
Directions:
Preheat broiler to 400 degrees f. Daintily oil a preparing sheet or coat with nonstick shower.
In an enormous bowl, consolidate panko and parmesan; season with salt and pepper, to taste. Put in a safe spot.
Working in clumps, dig zucchini adjusts in flour, dunk into eggs, at that point dig in panko blend, squeezing to cover.
Spot zucchini in a solitary layer onto the readied heating sheet. Spot into stove and heat until delicate and brilliant dark-colored, around 18 to 20 minutes.
Top with marinara and mozzarella.
At that point cook for 2 to 3minutes, or until the cheddar has dissolved.
Servings quickly, embellished with parsley, whenever wanted.
Nutrition: Calories: 217;carbs: 21g;fat: 12g;protein:

Grilled Fig And Peach Arugula Salad With Ricotta Salute And A Black Pepper Vinagretteprint

Preparation Time: 10 minutes
Cooking Time: 20 Minutes
Servings: 2
Ingredients:
Dressing:
3 - tablespoons good-quality olive oil
1 - teaspoon good balsamic vinegar
½ lemon from juice
Salt
6 to 7 - turns freshly ground pepper
Salad:
4 - figs, halved
1 - teaspoon dark brown sugar
Salt
Olive oil
Few handfuls of arugulas, 2 ounces, cleaned and dried
1 - yellow peach, sliced
3 to 4 - pistachios, chopped
2 - slices prosciutto
Ricotta salata
Directions:
In a little bowl, including the olive oil, balsamic vinegar, lemon juice, squeeze of salt and naturally ground pepper; blend until altogether joined. Do a trial and include more salt, in the event that you like. Put in a safe spot.
Sprinkle the figs with the dim dark colored sugar and a touch of salt. Warmth a barbecue or flame broil skillet. Whenever hot, brush with olive oil. Spot the figs on the hot flame broil, face down and cook for 1-minutes, until barbecue imprints show up. Expel and put in a safe spot.
To a huge blending bowl, include the arugula. Sprinkle the leaves with salt. Include half of the dressing and delicately prepare the serving of mixed greens. Move the lettuce to your serving plate. Add the peaches to the blending bowl and hurl with a touch of dressing. Move the peaches and figs to the serving plate, masterminding anyway you like. Top with a sprinkling of pistachios, a couple of torn bits of prosciutto and slight cuts of ricotta salata.
Nutrition: Calories: 3;carbs: 26g;fat: 24g;protein: 10g

Honey Mustard Pork Tenderloin

Preparation time: 10 minutes
Cooking time: 26 minutes
Servings: 1
Ingredients

- 1 lb. pork tenderloin
- 1 tsp. sriracha sauce
- 1 tbsp. garlic, minced
- 2 tbsps. soy sauce
- 1 ½ tbsp. honey
- ¾ tbsp. Dijon mustard
- 1 tbsp. mustard

Directions

1. Add sriracha sauce, garlic, soy sauce, honey, Dijon mustard, and mustard into the large zip-lock bag and mix well.
2. Add pork tenderloin into the bag.
3. Seal bag and place in the refrigerator overnight.
4. Preheat the air fryer oven to 380°F.
5. Spray air fryer tray with cooking spray, then place marinated pork tenderloin on a tray and air fry for 26 minutes.
6. Turn pork tenderloin after every 5 minutes.
7. Slice and serve.

Nutrition

- Calories: 195 kcal.
- Fat: 4.1 g.
- Carbs: 8 g.
- Proten: 30.5 g.

Chicken Simmered With Black Beans

Preparation time: 10 minutes
Cooking time: 30 minutes
Servings: 3
Ingredients

- ½ tsp. olive oil
- 6 oz. skinless chicken breasts, cubed
- 1 tsp. curry powder
- ½ tsp. ground cumin
- ½ tsp. garlic powder
- ½ tsp. paprika
- ¼ tsp. red pepper flakes
- ¼ tsp. freshly ground black pepper
- 2 tbsps. low sodium chicken stock
- Juice of 1 lime
- ¼ C. canned black beans, drained and rinsed

Directions

1. Heat the olive oil in a large non-stick pan over medium heat and sear the chicken cubes until browned on all sides.
2. Add the curry powder, ground cumin, garlic powder, paprika, red pepper flakes, black pepper, chicken stock, and lime juice to the pan.
3. Cover the pan with a lid, cook over medium-low heat for another 10–15 minutes or until the chicken is cooked through.
4. Add the black beans to the pan, and simmer covered for 5 minutes until the beans are heated through.

Nutrition

- Calories: 144 kcal.
- Protein: 22 g.
- Total carbs: 8 g.
- Dietary fiber: 3 g.
- Total fat: 5 g.

Greek Baked Chicken

Preparation time: 10 minutes
Cooking time: 20 minutes
Servings: 3
Ingredients

- Olive oil cooking spray
- 2 ripe beef tomatoes finely chopped
- 1 tbsp. balsamic vinegar
- 2 small skinless chicken breasts
- 2 tsps. minced garlic
- 1 tbsp. dried oregano
- 1 tsp. chopped chives
- ½ C. reduced-sodium chicken stock
- ¼ C. reduced-sodium green olives stuffed with pimiento, thickly sliced

Directions

1. Preheat the oven to 400°F.
2. Spray an ovenproof dish with cooking spray.
3. Marinate the tomatoes with balsamic vinegar and set them aside.
4. Rub the chicken breasts with minced garlic, dried oregano, and chives.
5. Pour the chicken stock into the oven dish and arrange the chicken breasts in the dish.
6. Bake for 20 minutes.
7. Remove the dish from the oven and reduce the temperature to 350°F.
8. Flip over the chicken breasts and add the marinated tomatoes and olives to the dish.
9. Return to the oven for another 20–25 minutes, or until the chicken is cooked through and the tomatoes are softened.

Nutrition
- Calories: 177 kcal.
- Protein: 23 g.
- Total carbs: 13 g.
- Dietary fiber: 1 g.
- Total fat: 4 g.

Sweet and Tangy Chicken With Pumpkin Purée

Preparation time: 10 minutes
Cooking time: 30 minutes
Servings: 3

Ingredients
- Zest and juice of 1 lime
- 1 tbsp. bacon root syrup
- 2 tbsps. chopped lemongrass, and 1 stalk lemongrass, bruised
- 2 small skinless chicken breasts
- 1 tbsp. oil
- ½ C. canned pumpkin purée

Directions

To make the marinade:
1. Mix the lime zest, lime juice, bacon root syrup, chopped lemongrass in a bowl, and set aside.
2. Make a few scores on each chicken breast with a sharp knife.
3. Rub the marinade onto the chicken breasts, taking care to also rub it into the scores. This will help the meat absorb more of the flavor.
4. Set aside to rest for 15 minutes. Meantime, preheat the grill/broiler, and line the grill tray with foil.
5. Grill the chicken breasts for 10–15 minutes or until they are cooked through.
6. Remove from the grill and set aside for the meat to rest.

To make the pumpkin purée:
1. Heat the oil in a small frying pan over low heat, and lightly fry the lemongrass stalk until its fragrance is released.
2. Stir in the pumpkin purée and allow to cook for a few minutes until the purée is heated through.
3. Discard the lemongrass stalk.
4. Divide the pumpkin purée between 2 plates and arrange the chicken breasts on the top to serve.

Nutrition
- Calories: 171 kcal.
- Protein: 20 g.
- Total carbs: 8 g.
- Dietary fiber: 2 g.
- Total fat: 5 g.

Country Style Pork Tenderloin

Preparation time: 15 minutes
Cooking time: 25 minutes
Servings: 1
Ingredients

- 1 lb. pork tenderloin
- 1 tbsp. garlic, minced
- 2 tbsps. soy sauce
- 2 tbsps. honey
- 1 tbsp. Dijon mustard
- 1 tbsp. grain mustard
- 1 tsp. Sriracha sauce

Directions

1. In a large bowl, add all the ingredients except pork and mix well.
2. Add the pork tenderloin and coat with the mixture generously.
3. Refrigerate to marinate for 2–3 hours.
4. Remove the pork tenderloin from the bowl, reserving the marinade.
5. Place the pork tenderloin onto the lightly greased cooking tray.
6. Arrange the drip pan in the bottom of the Air Fryer Oven cooking chamber.
7. Select "Air Fry" and then adjust the temperature to 380°F.
8. Set the timer for 25 minutes and press the "Start."
9. When the display shows "Add Food" insert the cooking tray in the center position.
10. When the display shows "Turn Food" turn the pork and oat with the reserved marinade.
11. When cooking time is complete, remove the tray from Air fryer oven and place the pork tenderloin onto a platter for about 10 minutes before slicing.
12. With a sharp knife, cut the pork tenderloin into desired-sized slices and serve.

Nutrition

- Calories: 277 kcal.
- Fat: 5.7 g.
- Carbs: 14.2 g.

Protein: 40.7 g.

Simple Beef Sirloin Roast

Preparation time: 10 minutes
Cooking time: 50 minutes
Servings: 1
Ingredients

- 2 ½ lbs. sirloin roast
- 1 tsp. salt and ground black pepper, as required

Directions

1. Rub the roast with salt and black pepper generously. Insert the rotisserie rod through the roast. Insert the rotisserie forks, one on each side of the rod to secure the rod to the chicken. Arrange the drip pan in the bottom of the Air Fryer Oven cooking chamber.
2. Select "Roast" and then adjust the temperature to 350°F.
3. Set the timer for 50 minutes and press the "Start."
4. When the display shows "Add Food" press the red lever down and load the left side of the rod into the air fryer oven.
5. Now, slide the rod's left side into the groove along the metal bar so it doesn't move. Then, close the door and touch "Rotate."
6. Press the red lever to release the rod when cooking time is complete.
7. Remove from the Air fryer oven and place the roast onto a platter for about 10 minutes before slicing. With a sharp knife, cut the roast into desired-sized slices and serve.

Nutrition

- Calories: 201 kcal.
- Fat: 8.8 g.
- Carbs: 0 g.
- Protein: 28.9 g.

Shrimp, Zucchini and Cherry Tomato Sauce

Preparation time: 5 minutes
Cooking time: 30 minutes
Servings: 1
Ingredients

- 2 zucchinis
- 300 shrimps
- 7 cherry tomatoes
- 1 tsp. salt and pepper to taste
- 1 clove garlic

Directions

1. Pour oil into the air fryer, add garlic clove, and diced zucchini.
2. Cook for 15 minutes at 1500°C.
3. Add the shrimp and the pieces of tomato, salt, and spices.
4. Cook for another 5–10 minutes or until the shrimp water evaporates.

Nutrition

- Calories: 214.3 kcal.
- Fat: 8.6 g.
- Carbohydrate: 7.8 g.
- Sugars: 4.8 g.
- Protein: 27.0 g.
- Cholesterol: 232.7 mg.

Baked Parmesan and Herb Coated Chicken Strips

Preparation time: 10 minutes
Cooking time: 40 minutes
Servings: 3
Ingredients

- 1 oz. low-fat Parmesan cheese, grated
- ¼ C. whole wheat bread-crumbs
- 1 tsp. dried basil
- 1 tsp. dried oregano
- 1 tsp. dried thyme
- ½ tsp. paprika
- ¼ tsp. sea salt
- 1 large egg, white only
- 6 oz. skinless chicken breasts, sliced into the 1-inch-thick strip

Directions

1. Preheat the oven to 400°F and line a baking sheet with parchment paper.
2. Combine the grated Parmesan cheese with bread crumbs, dried herbs, paprika, and sea salt.
3. Spread over a shallow dish.
4. Whisk the egg white and pour into another shallow dish.
5. Dredge the chicken strips in the whisked egg white, and then coat them evenly in the bread crumbs.
6. Arrange the chicken strips onto the baking sheet and bake for 15–20 minutes, or until the chicken is cooked through. Serve with a crispy lettuce salad.

Nutrition

- Calories: 236 kcal.
- Protein: 35 g.
- Total carbs: 13 g.
- Dietary fiber: 2 g.
- Total fat: 5 g.

Low-Carb Chicken Tortillas

Preparation time: *10 minutes*
Cooking time: *20 minutes*
Servings: *3*

Ingredients

- 1 tsp. olive oil cooking spray
- ¼ red pepper deseeded and sliced thinly
- ¼ yellow pepper deseeded and sliced thinly
- 6 oz. skinless chicken breasts, cut into thin strips
- ¼ tsp. paprika
- ¼ tsp. cumin
- ¼ tsp. dried oregano
- 2 low-carb tortillas
- 2 C. iceberg lettuce, finely shredded

Directions

1. Preheat the oven to 325°F.
2. Lightly spray a non-stick frying pan with the cooking spray, and heat over medium heat.
3. Add the peppers and sauté until they are softened.
4. Add the chicken, paprika, cumin, and dried oregano to the peppers.
5. Continue cooking for 15 minutes or until the chicken is cooked through. When the chicken is cooking, the tortillas can be wrapped in foil and warmed for 5 minutes.

To assemble:

1. Spoon half of the chicken into the center of each tortilla and top with 1 C. of shredded lettuce.
2. Roll the tortilla and serve warm.

Nutrition

- Calories: 196 kcal.
- Protein: 26 g.
- Total carbs: 3 g.
- Dietary fiber: 1 g.
- Total fat: 4 g.

Stuffed Chicken

Preparation time: *10 minutes*
Cooking time: *50 minutes*
Servings: *3*

Ingredients

- ½ C. fresh green beans, trimmed, blanched, and cooled
- ½ C. cherry tomatoes, halved
- ¼ red onion finely chopped
- ½ clove garlic, minced
- 1 tsp. balsamic vinegar
- Freshly ground black pepper, to taste
- 2 small skinless chicken breasts
- 2 tbsps. low-fat spreadable cheese

Directions

1. To make the green bean and tomato salad: Combine the green beans, cherry tomatoes, onions, garlic, and balsamic vinegar in a bowl.
2. Season well with freshly ground black pepper.
3. Set aside to chill for an hour.
4. Preheat the oven to 400°F and line a baking tray with parchment paper.
5. Cut a slit in the chicken breasts to form a pocket.
6. Season well with black pepper and stuff 1 tbsp.
7. Cheese into each cavity. Secure with a toothpick if needed.
8. Bake for 35–40 minutes, or until the chicken is cooked through.
9. Serve with the green bean and tomato salad.

Nutrition

- Calories: 140 kcal.
- Protein: 20 g.
- Total carbs: 7 g.
- Dietary fiber: 2 g.
- Total fat: 4 g.

Lean Spring Stew

Preparation Time: *15 minutes*
Cooking Time: *1 Hour 15 Minutes*

73

Servings: 4
Ingredients:
1 lb. diced fire roasted tomatoes
4 boneless, skinless chicken thighs
1 tbsp dried basil
8 oz chicken stock
Salt & pepper to taste
4 oz tomato paste
3 chopped celery stalks
3 chopped carrots
2 chili peppers, finely chopped
2 tbsp olive oil
1 finely chopped onion
2 garlic cloves, crushed
½ container mushroomsSour cream
Directions: Heat up the olive oil over medium-high temperature. Add the celery, onions and carrots and stir-fry for 5 to minutes. Transfer to a deep pot and add tomato paste, basil, garlic, mushrooms and seasoning. Keep stirring the vegetables until they are completely covered by tomato sauce. At the same time, cut the chicken into small cubes to make it easier to eat. Put the chicken in a deep pot, pour the chicken stock over it and throw in the tomatoes. Stir the chicken in to ensure the ingredients and vegetables are properly mixed with it. Turn the heat to low and cook for about an hour. The vegetables and chicken should be cooked through before you turn the heat off. Top with sour cream and serve!
Nutrition: Net carbs 19 g; Fiber 3 g;Fats 11.9 g;Fatsr 3 g;Calories 27

Yummy Chicken Bites

Preparation Time: 10 minutes
Cooking Time: 10 Minutes
Servings: 2
Ingredients:
1 lb chicken breasts, skinless, boneless and cut into cubes
2 tbsp fresh lemon juice
1 tbsp fresh oregano, chopped
2 tbsp olive oil
1/8 tsp cayenne pepper
Pepper
Salt
Directions:
Place chicken in a bowl.
Add reaming ingredients over chicken and mix well.
Place chicken in the refrigerator for 1 hour.
Heat grill over medium heat.
Spray grill with cooking spray.
Thread marinated chicken onto skewers.
Arrange skewers on grill and grill until chicken is cooked.
Serve and enjoy.
Nutrition:Per Servings: Calories 560 Fat 31 g Carbohydrates 1.8 g Sugar 0.4 g Protein 66 g Cholesterol 200 mg

Shrimp Scampi

Preparation Time: 5 minutes
Cooking Time: 10 Minutes
Servings: 4
Ingredients:
1 lb. Shrimp
1/4 tsp red pepper flakes
1 tbsp fresh lemon juice
1/4 cup butter
1/2 cup chicken broth
2 garlic cloves, minced
1 shallot, sliced
3 tbsp olive oil
3 tbsp parsley, chopped
Pepper
Salt
Directions:
Heat oil in a pan over medium heat.
Add garlic and shallots and cook for 3 minutes.
Add broth, lemon juice, and butter and cook for 5 minutes.
Add red pepper flakes, parsley, pepper, and salt. Stir.
Add shrimp and cook for 3 minutes.
Serve and enjoy.
Nutrition: Calories 336;Fat 24 g;Carbohydrates 3 g;Sugar 0.2 g;Protein 26 g;Cholesterol 269 mg

Zucchini Frittata

Preparation Time: 10 minutes
Cooking Time: 10 Minutes
Servings: 4
Ingredients:
2 teaspoons butter (divided)
1 cup shredded zucchini
Salt and freshly ground black pepper, to taste
4 eggs (lightly beaten)
2 tablespoons skim milk
1/4 teaspoon garlic salt
1/4 teaspoon onion powder
2 tablespoons shredded mild cheddar cheese
Directions:
In a medium nonstick skillet over medium heat, melt teaspoon butter and sauté zucchini until softened and lightly browned, 4 to 5 minutes, stirring frequently.
Drain zucchini if necessary and season to taste with salt and pepper. Beat eggs with milk, garlic salt, onion powder and zucchini until combined. Melt remaining 1 teaspoon butter in skillet, add egg mixture and cook until partially set. Lift edges of cooked egg with a spatula, let uncooked egg run underneath and continue until top of frittata is set, about 4 minutes.
Carefully flip frittata and let cook until lightly browned, to 4 minutes. Remove skillet from heat, sprinkle cheese over frittata and let stand until cheese is melted.
Cut frittata in half and serve immediately. Enjoy!
Nutrition:Per Serving:Calories: 20 Total Fat: 15g; Saturated Fat: 7g; Protein: 14g; Carbs: 4g; Fiber: 1g; Sugar: 3g

Salmon Patties

Preparation Time: 10 minutes
Cooking Time: 10 Minutes
Servings: 3
Ingredients:
14.5 oz can salmon
4 tbsp butter
1 avocado, diced
2 eggs, lightly beaten
1/2 cup almond flour
1/2 onion, minced
Pepper
Salt
Directions:
Add all ingredients except butter in a large mixing bowl and mix until well combined.
Make six patties from mixture. Set aside.
Melt butter in a pan over medium heat.
Place patties on pan and cook for 5 minutes on each side.
Serve and enjoy.
Nutrition: Calories 9;Fat 49 g;Carbohydrates 11 g;Sugar 2 g;Protein 36 g;Cholesterol 225 mg

Apple Cinnamon Oatmeal

Preparation Time: 10 minutes
Cooking Time: 10 Minutes
Servings: 1
Ingredients:
1/2 cup skim milk
1/3 cup water
1 apple (peeled, cored, diced)
Dash of salt
1/2 cup old fashioned oats
1/4 teaspoon cinnamon
1/4 teaspoon vanilla
Directions:
Mix milk, water, apple and salt in a small saucepan and heat to a simmer, stirring occasionally (do not boil).
Add oats and cinnamon to saucepan and simmer, uncovered, for about 5 minutes, stirring occasionally.
Stir vanilla into oatmeal and serve immediately. Enjoy!
Nutrition:Per Serving:Calories: 18 Total Fat: 2g; Saturated Fat: 0g; Protein: 7g; Carbs: 36g; Fiber: 4g; Sugar: 19g

Stuff Cheese Pork Chops

Preparation Time: 10 minutes
Cooking Time: 25 Minutes
Servings: 4
Ingredients:
4 pork chops, boneless and thick cut
2 tbsp olives, chopped
2 tbsp sun-dried tomatoes, chopped

½ cup feta cheese, crumbled
2 garlic cloves, minced
2 tbsp fresh parsley, chopped
Directions:
Preheat the oven to 375 f.
In a bowl, mix together feta cheese, garlic, parsley, olives, and sun-dried tomatoes.
Stuff feta cheese mixture in the pork chops. Season with pepper and salt.
Bake for 35 minutes.
Serve and enjoy.
Nutrition: Calories 31Fat 25 g;Carbohydrates 2 g;Sugar 1 g;Protein 21 g;Cholesterol 75 mg

• Italian Pork Chops

Preparation Time: 10 minutes
Cooking Time: 30 Minutes
Servings: 4
Ingredients:
4 pork loin chops, boneless
2 garlic cloves, minced
1 tsp Italian seasoning
1 tbsp fresh rosemary, chopped
1/4 tsp black pepper
1/2 tsp kosher salt
Directions:
Season pork chops with pepper and salt.
In a small bowl, mix together garlic, Italian seasoning, and rosemary.
Rub pork chops with garlic and rosemary mixture.
Place pork chops on a baking tray and roast in oven at 5 f for 10 minutes.
Turn temperature to 3 f and roast for 25 minutes more
Serve and enjoy.
Nutrition: Calories 261;Fat 19 g;Carbohydrates 2 g;Sugar 0 g;Protein 18 g;Cholesterol 68 mg;Fiber 0.4 g;Net carbs 1 g

• Sunshine Wrap

Preparation Time: 10 minutes
Cooking Time: 30 Minutes
Servings: 2
Ingredients:
8 oz. Grilled chicken breast
½ c. Diced celery
2/3 c. Mandarin oranges
¼ c. Minced onion
2 tbsps. Mayonnaise
1 tsp. Soy sauce
¼ tsp. Garlic powder
¼ tsp. Black pepper
1 whole wheat tortilla
4 lettuce leaves
Directions:
Combine all ingredients, except tortilla and lettuce, in a large bowl and toss to evenly coat.
Lay tortillas on a flat surface and cut into quarters.
Top each quarter with a lettuce leaf and spoon chicken mixture into the middle of each.
Roll each tortilla into a cone and seal by slightly wetting the edge with water. Enjoy!
Nutrition: Calories: 280.8, Fat: 21.1g, Carbs: 3g, Protein: 19g

Taco Omelet

Preparation Time: 10 minutes
Cooking Time: 10 Minutes
Servings: 1
Ingredients:
2 eggs (lightly beaten)
2 tablespoons skim milk
1/4 teaspoon chili powder
1/4 teaspoon garlic powder
1/4 teaspoon onion powder
Salt and freshly ground black pepper, to taste
1 teaspoon vegetable oil
1 tablespoon guacamole
1 tablespoon sour cream
1 tablespoon salsa
2 tablespoons shredded cojack cheese
Directions:
In a medium bowl, whisk eggs, milk, chili powder, garlic powder and onion powder and season to taste with salt and pepper.
Heat oil in a medium nonstick skillet over medium heat. Pour egg mixture into skillet and swirl to coat evenly. Cover skillet and let eggs cook until set on top, about 4 minutes.
With a large spatula, carefully flip omelet. Season omelet to taste with salt and pepper and let cook until lightly browned on the bottom, about minutes more.
Slide omelet onto a plate. Spread guacamole, sour cream and salsa all over one side of the omelet and sprinkle with cheese. Fold omelet in half over filling and serve immediately. Enjoy
Nutrition:Per Serving:Calories: 290; Total Fat: 22g; Saturated Fat: 10g; Protein: 17g; Carbs: 6g; Fiber: 1g; Sugar: 3g

Sheet Pan Spicy Tofu And Green Beans

Preparation Time: 10 minutes
Cooking Time: 30 Minutes
Servings: 4
Ingredients:
Spicy marinade:
1 - teaspoon minced garlic
1/4 - cup sliced scallions
2 - teaspoons sesame seeds, plus more for garnish
3 - tablespoons soy sauce
1 - tablespoon sesame oil
1 - teaspoon red pepper flakes
1/2 - teaspoon maple syrup
2 - tablespoons of rice wine vinegar
16 - ounces firm tofu, drained and pressed
1 - pound green beans, trimmed
2 - teaspoons olive oil, for oiling the pan
Salt/pepper
Directions:
Preheat the broiler to 400 degrees f.
Flush and channel your tofu, at that point press utilizing a tofu press or envelop by paper towels and spot overwhelming books or dish on top. Let channel for in any event 10 to 15 minutes, this will enable the marinade to be assimilated.
Whisk together the elements for the zesty sauce.
Cut the tofu into triangles and spot in a solitary layer on an oiled preparing sheet. Shower with the hot sauce at that point prepares for 12 minutes.
Flip tofu and sprinkle with more sauce. Add the green beans to the opposite side of the container in a solitary layer, as would be prudent. Shower with residual sauce and sprinkle with salt and pepper.
Return back to the stove and heat until tofu is caramelized and somewhat fresh, around 12-15 minutes.
Sprinkle with residual sesame seeds, whenever wanted, and serve.
Nutrition: Calories: 21carbs: 20g;fat: 11g;protein: 12g

Skillet Chicken Thighs With Potato, Apple, And Spinach

Preparation Time: 10 minutes
Cooking Time: 20 Minutes
Servings: 1
Ingredients:
1 - small chicken thigh
Salt
Pepper
1 - teaspoon canola oil
1 - medium russet potato, cut into 1/2 inch cubes
1 - small fuji apple, cored and cut into 6 wedges
1 - teaspoon fresh sage, chopped

1 - cup packed baby spinach
Directions:
Warm broiler to 400°.
Season bird generously with salt and pepper.
In an extensive, broiler-secure skillet over medium warmth, warmness oil. Include bird, skin side down, and prepare dinner till pores and skin crisps marginally and a few fats are rendered round minutes. Include potato, apple, and sage. Toss to cowl and arrange potato and apple around the skillet, making sure hen is skin side down.
Move skillet to broiler and dish 15 minutes. Flip chicken, at that factor, broil 10 minutes extra, till potatoes and apples are delicate and chicken is cooked thru with no red within the middle.
Return skillet to stovetop over medium-low heat. Take off the chicken, consist of spinach and hurl with potatoes and apples to shrivel.
Top vegetable mixture with chook to serve.
Nutrition: Calories 514;fat 22g;carbs 59g;sugar 23g;protein 21g

- **Cherry Tomatoes Tilapia Salad**

Preparation Time: 10 minutes
Cooking Time: 25 Minutes
Servings: 3
Ingredients:
1 c. Mixed greens
1 c. Cherry tomatoes
1/3 c. Diced red onion
1 medium avocado
3 tortilla crusted tilapia fillet
Directions:
Spray tilapia fillet with a little bit of cooking spray. Put fillets in air fryer basket. Cook for minutes at about 390° f.
Transfer the fillet to a bowl. Toss with tomatoes, greens and red onion. Add the lime dressing and mix again.
Serve and enjoy!
Nutrition: Calories: 271, fat: 8g, carbs: 10.1g, protein: 18.5g

Apple Cider Glazed Chicken Breast With Carrots

Preparation Time: 10 minutes
Cooking Time: 6hrs 45 Minutes
Servings: 2
Ingredients:
2 - boneless skin-on chicken breasts
2 - cups apple cider
4 - whole peppercorns
2 - small bunches of fresh sage
½ - teaspoon salt
2 - tablespoons olive oil
Salt and pepper, to taste
4 - carrots, peeled and sliced
1 - tablespoon butter
Directions:
To start with, in all probability, your boneless skin-on chicken bosom still has the tenderloin connected. Expel (it's the additional piece that resembles a chicken strip). This helps the chicken cooks quicker. I solidify the tenderloins for soup or make chicken strips with them.
In an enormous dish or bowl, include the chicken, apple juice, peppercorns, sage (torn and hacked first), and ½ teaspoon of salt. Let marinate shrouded in the cooler for at least 4hrs.
Following 4hrs, expel the chicken and pat the chicken dry. Warm the oil in a huge skillet. At the point when the oil is hot, sprinkle the chicken with additional salt and pepper and spot its skin-side down in the container. Cook on both side until brilliant darker.
In the meantime, strip and bones the carrots. Spot them in a microwave-safe bowl, spread with saran wrap and microwave for 1 moment.
Take the flavors out from the apple juice, and after that pour it over the chicken once the two sides are brilliant dark colored. Change the warmth so the apple juice goes to a stew and cook until the chicken registers 16degrees f on a thermometer. Evacuate the chicken and put aside when done.
When the chicken is done, turn the warmth to high and lessen the apple juice to a thick coat. Include the carrots and saute for 3 to 4 minutes, until fresh delicate. Include the spread before expelling them from the dish. Mix to cover the carrots in the coating and margarine. Utilize any additional coating from the dish to brush on the chicken and serve the chicken with the carrots.
Nutrition: Calories: 328;fat: 20g;carbs: 39g;sugar: 2;protein: 2g

• Onion Paprika Pork Tenderloin

Preparation Time: 10 minutes
Cooking Time: 30 Minutes
Servings: 6
Ingredients:
2 lbs. Pork tenderloin
For rub
1 1/2 tbsp smoked paprika
1 tbsp garlic powder
1 1/2 tbsp onion powder
½ tbsp salt
Directions:
Preheat the oven to 425 f.
In a small bowl, mix together all rub ingredients and rub over pork tenderloin.
Spray pan with cooking spray and heat over medium-high heat.
Sear pork on all sides until lightly golden brown.
Place pan into the oven and roast for about 230 minutes.
Sliced and serve.
Nutrition: Calories 225;Fat 5 g;Carbohydrates 2 g;Sugar 1 g;Protein 41 g;Cholesterol 45 mg

• Rosemary Garlic Pork Chops

Preparation Tim: 10 minutes
Cooking Time: 35 Minutes
Servings: 4
Ingredients:
4 pork chops, boneless
¼ tsp onion powder
2 garlic cloves, minced
1 tsp dried rosemary, crushed
¼ tsp pepper
¼ tsp sea salt
Directions:
Preheat the oven to 425 f.
Season pork chops with onion powder, pepper and salt.

Mix together rosemary and garlic and rub over pork chops.

Place pork chops on baking tray and roast for 10 minutes.

Set temperature 3 f and roast for 25 minutes more. Serve and enjoy.

Nutrition: Calories 260;Fat 20 g;Carbohydrates 1 g;Sugar 0 g;Protein 19 g;Cholesterol mg

Skinny Chicken Pesto Bake

Preparation Time: 10 minutes
Cooking Time: 35 Minutes
Servings: 4
Ingredients:
160 oz. Skinless chicken
1 tsps. Basil
1 sliced tomato
6 tbsps. Shredded mozzarella cheese
2 tsps. Grated parmesan cheese
Directions:
Cut chicken into thin strips.

Set oven to 400 degrees f. Prepare a baking sheet by lining with parchment paper.

Lay chicken strips on prepared baking sheet. Top with pesto and brush evenly over chicken pieces.

Set to bake until chicken is fully cooked (about 15 minutes).

Garnish with parmesan cheese, mozzarella, and tomatoes.

Set to continue baking until cheese melts (about 5 minutes).

Nutrition: Calories: 205, fat: 8.5g, carbs: 2.5g, protein: 30g

Cold Tomato Couscous

Preparation Time: 10 mnutes
Cooking Time: 10 Minutes
Servings: 4
Ingredients:
5 oz couscous
3 tbsp tomato sauce
3 tbsp lemon juice
1 small-sized onion, chopped
1 cup vegetable stock
½ small-sized cucumber, sliced
½ small-sized carrot, sliced
¼ tsp salt3 tbsp olive oil
½ cup fresh parsley, chopped
Directions:
First, pour the couscous into a large bowl. Boil the vegetable broth and slightly add in the couscous while stirring constantly. Leave it for about minutes until couscous absorbs the liquid. Cover with a lid and set aside. Stir from time to time to speed up the soaking process and break the lumps with a spoon.

Meanwhile, preheat the olive oil in a frying pan, and add the tomato sauce. Add chopped onion and stir until translucent. Set aside and let it cool for a few minutes.

Add the oily tomato sauce to the couscous and stir well. Now add lemon juice, chopped parsley, and salt to the mixture and give it a final stir.

Serve with sliced cucumber, carrot, and parsley.
Nutrition:Per Serving:Net carbs 32.8 g;Fiber 3.2 g;Fats 11 g;Fatsr 6 g;Calories 249

Fresh Shrimp Spring Rolls

Preparation Time: 10 minutes
Cooking Time: 20 minutes
Servings: 12
Ingredients:
12 sheets rice paper
12 bib lettuce
12 basil laves
¾ c. cilantro
1 c. shredded carrots
½ sliced cucumber
20 oz. cooked shrimp
Directions:
Add all vegetables and shrimp to separate bowls.

Set a damp paper towel tower flat on work surface.

Quickly wet a sheet of rice papers under warm water and lay on paper towel.

Top with 1 of each vegetable and 4 pieces of shrimp, then roll in rice paper into a burrito – like roll.

Repeat until all vegetables and shrimp has been used up. Serve and enjoy.

Nutritional Information:
Calories: 67, Fat: 2.9g, Carbs: 7.4g, Protein: 2.6g

Chicken Breast Tortilla

Preparation Time: 10 minutes
Cooking Time: 30 minutes
Servings: 2
Ingredients:
8 oz. grilled chicken breast
½ c. diced celery
2/3 c. mandarin oranges
¼ c. minced onion
2 tbsps. mayonnaise
1 tsp. soy sauce
¼ tsp. garlic powder
¼ tsp. black pepper
1 whole wheat tortilla
4 lettuce leaves
Directions:
Combine all ingredients, except tortilla and lettuce, in a large bowl and toss to evenly coat.
Lay tortillas on a flat surface and cut into quarters. Top each quarter with a lettuce leaf and spoon chicken mixture into the middle of each.
Roll each tortilla into a cone and seal by slightly wetting the edge with water. Enjoy!
Nutritional Information:
Calories: 280.8, Fat: 21.1g, Carbs: 3g, Protein: 19g

Sweet Roasted Beet & Arugula Tortilla Pizza V

Preparation Time: 10 minutes
Cooking Time: 25 minutes
Servings: 6
Ingredients:
2 chopped Beets
6 Corn Tortillas
1 c. Arugula
½ c. Goat cheese
1 c. Blackberries
2 tbsps. Honey
2 tbsps. Balsamic vinegar
Directions:
Preheat oven to 350 F. Lay tortillas on a flat surface. Top with beets, berries and goat cheese. Combine balsamic vinegar and honey together in a small bowl, and whisk to combine.
Drizzle the mixture over pizza and to bake for about 10 minutes, or until cheese has melted slightly and tortilla is crisp.
Garnish with arugula and serve.
Nutritional Information:
Calories: 286, Fat: 40g, Carbs: 42g, Protein: 15g

Southwestern Black Bean Cakes with Guacamole

Preparation Time: 10 minutes
Cooking Time: 25 minutes
Servings: 4
Ingredients:
1 c. whole wheat bread crumbs
3 tbsps. chopped cilantro
2 garlic cloves
15 oz. black beans
7 oz. chipotle peppers in adobo sauce
1 tsp. ground cumin
1 large egg
½ diced avocado
1 tbsp. lime juice
1 tomato plum
Directions:
Drain beans and add all ingredients, except avocado, lime juice and eggs, to a food processor and run until the mixture begins to pull away from the sides.
Transfer to a large bowl and add egg, then mix well.
Form into 4 even patties and cook on a preheated, greased grill over medium heat for about 10 minutes, flipping halfway through.
Add avocado and lime juice in a small bowl, then stir and mash together using a fork.
Season to taste then serve with bean cakes.
Nutritional Information:
Calories: 178, Fat: 7g, Carbs: 25g, Protein: 11g

Veggie Quesadillas with Cilantro Yogurt Dip

Preparation Time: 10 minutes
Cooking Time: 25 minutes
Servings: 3
Ingredients:
1 c. black beans

2 tbsps. chopped cilantro
½ chopped bell pepper
½ c. corn kernels
1 c. shredded cheese
6 corn tortillas
1 shredded carrot
Instructions:
Set skillet to preheat on low heat. Lay 3 tortillas on a flat surface.
Top evenly with peppers, carrots, cilantro, beans, corn and cheese over the tortillas, covering each with another tortilla, maximum.
Add quesadilla to preheated skillet. Cook until the cheese melts and tortilla is a nice golden brown (about 2 min).
Flip quesadilla and cook for about a minute or until golden.
Mix well. Slice each quesadilla into 4 even wedges and serve with dip. Enjoy!
Nutritional Information:
Calories: 344, Fat: 8g, Carbs: 46g, Protein: 27g

- **Mayo-less Tuna Salad**

Preparation Time: 10 minutes
Cooking Time: 5 minutes
Servings: 2
Ingredients:
5 oz. tuna
1 tbsp. olive oil
1 tbsp. red wine vinegar
¼ c. chopped green onion
2 c. arugula
1 c. cooked pasta
1 tbsp. parmesan cheese
Black pepper
Directions:
Combine all ingredients into a medium bowl. Split mixture between two plates. Serve, and enjoy.
Nutritional Information:
Calories: 213.2, Fat: 6.2g, Carbs: 20.3g, Protein: 22.7g

Southwest Style Zucchini Rice Bowl

Preparation Time: 10 minutes
Cooking Time: 12 minutes
Servings: 2
Ingredients:
1 tbsp. vegetable oil
1 c. chopped vegetables
1 c. chopped chicken breast
1 c. cooked zucchini rice
4 tbsps. salsa
2 tbsps. shredded cheddar cheese
2 tbsps. sour cream
Directions:
Set a skillet with oil to heat up over medium heat.
Add chopped vegetables and allow to cook, stirring until vegetables become fork tender.
Add chicken and zucchini rice. Cook while stirring, until fully heated through.
Split between 2 serving bowls and garnish with remaining ingredients. Serve and enjoy!
Nutritional Information:
Calories: 168, Fat: 8.2g, Carbs: 18g, Protein: 5.5g

- **Pesto & Mozzarella Stuffed Portobello Mushroom Caps**

Preparation Time: 10 minutes
Cooking Time: 30 minutes
Servings: 2
Ingredients:
2 portobello mushrooms
1 diced Roma tomato
2 tbsps. pesto
¼ c. shredded mozzarella cheese
Directions:
Spoon pesto evenly into mushroom caps, then top with remaining ingredients.
Bake at 400 degrees F for about 15 minutes. Enjoy!
Nutritional Information:
Calories: 112, Fat: 5.4g, Carbs: 7.5g, Protein: 10.5g

Tandoori Chicken

Preparation Time: 10 minutes
Cooking Time: 35 minutes
Servings: 6
Ingredients:
1 c. plain yogurt
½ c, lemon juice
5 crushed garlic cloves
2 tbsps. paprika
1 tsp. yellow curry powder
1 tsp. ground ginger
6 skinless chicken breasts
6 skewers
Directions:
Set oven to 400 degrees F. In blender, combine red pepper flakes, ginger, curry, paprika, garlic, lemon juice and yogurt, then process into a smooth paste.
Add chicken strips evenly onto skewers. Add chicken to a shallow casserole dish then cover with ½ of yogurt mixture.
Tightly seal and rest in refrigerator for about 15 minutes.
Lightly grease a baking tray, then transfer chicken skewers onto it, and top with remaining yogurt mixture.
Set to bake until the chicken is fully cooked. Serve and enjoy.
Nutritional Information:
Calories: 177, Fat: 7.2g, Carbs: 6g, Protein: 20.6g

Turkey Fajitas Bowls

Preparation Time: 10 minutes
Cooking Time: 20 minutes
Servings: 4
Ingredients:
½ lb. turkey breast
2 tbsps. olive oil
1 tbsp. lemon juice
1 crushed garlic
¾ tsp. chopped chili pepper
½ tsp. dried oregano
1 sliced bell pepper
1 medium tomato
½ c. shredded cheddar cheese
4 tostada bowls
4 tbsps. salsa
Directions:
Add oregano, chili pepper, garlic, lemon juice and 1tbsp. olive oil to a medium bowl. Whisk to combine.
Add turkey then toss to coat. Allow to marinate for about 30 min.
Set a skillet over medium heat with remaining oil. Add bell pepper and allow to cook for 2 minutes, stirring.
Add turkey and cook for 3 more minutes. Add tomato, stir and remove from heat.
Spoon mixture evenly into tostada bowls.
Garnish with cheese and salsa then serve.
Nutritional Information:
Calories: 240, Fat: 15g, Carbs: 5g, Protein: 23g

Baked Chicken Pesto

Preparation Time: 10 minutes
Cooking Time: 35 minutes
Servings: 4
Ingredients:
160 oz. skinless chicken
1 tsps. basil
1 sliced tomato
6 tbsps. shredded mozzarella cheese
2 tsps. grated parmesan cheese
Directions:
Cut chicken into thin strips.
Set oven to 400 degrees F. Prepare a baking sheet by lining with parchment paper.
Lay chicken strips on prepared baking sheet. Top with pesto and brush evenly over chicken pieces.
Set to bake until chicken is fully cooked (about 15 minutes).
Garnish with parmesan cheese, mozzarella, and tomatoes.
Set to continue baking until cheese melts (about 5 minutes).
Nutritional Information:
Calories: 205, Fat: 8.5g, Carbs: 2.5g, Protein: 30g

Spaghetti Squash Lasagna V

Preparation Time: 10 minutes
Cooking Time: 1 hour 50 minutes
Servings: 6
Ingredients:

2 c. marinara sauce
3 c. roasted spaghetti squash
1 c. ricotta
8 tsps. grated parmesan cheese
6 oz. shredded mozzarella cheese
¼ tsp. red pepper flakes

Directions:

Set oven to preheat oven to 375 degrees F and spoon half of marinara sauce into baking dish.

Top with squash, then layer remaining ingredients.

Cover and set to bake until cheese is melted and edges brown (about 20 minutes).

Remove cover and return to bake for another 5 minutes. Enjoy!

Nutritional Information:
Calories: 255, Fat: 15.9g, Carbs: 5.5g, Protein: 21.4g

Crab Mushrooms

Preparation Time: 10 minutes
Cooking Time: 20 minutes
Servings: 5
Ingredients:
5 oz. crab meat
5 oz. white mushrooms
½ tsp. salt
¼ c. fish stock
1 tsp. butter
¼ tsp. ground coriander
1 tsp. dried cilantro
1 tsp. butter

Directions:

Chop the crab meat and sprinkle with salt and dried cilantro.

Mix the crab meat carefully. Preheat the air fryer to 400 F.

Chop the white mushrooms and combine with crab meat.

Add fish stock, ground coriander and butter.

Transfer the side dish mixture into the air fryer basket tray.

Stir gently with the help of a plastic spatula.

Cook the side dish for 5 minutes.

Rest for 5 minutes. Serve and enjoy!

Nutritional Information:
Calories: 56, Fat: 1.7g, Carbs: 2.6g, Protein: 7g

Loaded Sweet Potatoes

Preparation Time: 15 minutes
Cooking Time: 35 minutes
Servings: 4
Ingredients:
4 medium sweet potatoes, baked
½ c. Greek yogurt
1 tsp. taco seasoning
1 tsp. olive oil
1 diced red pepper
½ diced red onion
1 1/3 c. canned black beans
½ c. Mexican cheese blend
¼ c. chopped cilantro
½ c. salsa

Directions:

Mix taco seasoning and yogurt well, then set aside.

Set a skillet over medium heat with oil to get hot.

Add in remaining ingredients, except potatoes, cheese and salsa, and cook for about 8 minutes or until fully heated through.

Slightly pierce potatoes down the center and top evenly with all remaining ingredients. Serve.

Nutritional Information:
Calories: 311, Fat: 8.3g, Carbs: 57g, Protein: 3.2g

Coconut Flour Spinach Casserole

Preparation Time: 10 minutes
Cooking Time: 1 hour
Servings: 6
Ingredients:
4 eggs
¾ c. unsweetened almond milk
3 oz. chopped spinach
3 oz. chopped artichoke hearts
1 c. grated parmesan
3 minced garlic cloves
1 tsp. salt
½ tsp. pepper
¾ c. coconut flour
1 tbsp. baking powder
Directions:
Preheat air fryer to 375 degrees F. Grease air fryer pan with cooking spray.
Whisk eggs with almond milk, spinach, artichoke hearts and ½ cup of parmesan cheese. Add salt, garlic and pepper.
Add the coconut flour and baking powder; whisk until well combined.
Spread mixture into air fryer pan and sprinkle remaining cheese over it.
Place the baking pan in the air fryer and cook for about 30 minutes.
Remove baking pan from air fryer and sprinkle with chopped basil. Slice, then serve and enjoy!
Nutritional Information:
Calories: 175.2, Fat: 10.3g, Carbs: 2.4g, Protein: 17.7g

Tilapia With Cherry Tomatoes

Preparation Time: 10 minutes
Cooking Time: 25 minutes
Servings: 3
Ingredients:
1 c. mixed greens
1 c. cherry tomatoes
1/3 c. diced red onion
1 medium avocado
3 tortilla crusted tilapia fillet
Directions:
Spray tilapia fillet with a little bit of cooking spray. Put fillets in air fryer basket. Cook for 18 minutes at about 390° F.
Transfer the fillet to a bowl. Toss with tomatoes, greens and red onion. Add the lime dressing and mix again. Serve and enjoy!
Nutritional Information:
Calories: 271, Fat: 8g, Carbs: 10.1g, Protein: 18.5

Strawberry Frozen Yogurt Squares

Preparation Time: 10 minutes
Cooking Time: 8 hours
Servings: 8
Ingredients:
1 c. barley & wheat cereal
3 c. fat-free strawberry yogurt
10 oz. frozen strawberries
1 c. fat-free milk
1 c. whipped topping
Directions:
Set a parchment paper on the baking tray.
Spread cereal evenly over the bottom of the tray.
Add milk, strawberries and yogurt to blender, and process into a smooth mixture.
Use yogurt mixture to top cereal, wrap with foil, and place to freeze until firm (about 8 hours).
Slightly thaw, slice into squares and serve.
Nutritional Information:
Calories: 188, Fat: 0g, Carbs: 43.4g, Protein: 4.6g

Smoked Tofu Quesadillas

Preparation Time: 10 minutes
Cooking Time: 25 minutes
Servings: 4
Ingredients:
1 lb. extra firm sliced tofu
12 tortillas
2 tbsps. coconut oil
6 slices cheddar cheese
2 tbsps. sundried tomatoes
1 tbsp. cilantro
5 tbsps. sour cream
Directions:

Lay one tortilla flat and fill with tofu, tomato, cheese and top with oil. Repeat for as many as you need. Bake for 5 minutes and remove from flame.
Top with sour cream.
Nutritional Information:
Calories: 136, Fat: 6g, Carbs: 13g, Protein: 10g

• Zucchini Pizza Boats

Preparation Time: 10 minutes
Cooking Time: 45 minutes
Servings: 2
Ingredients:
2 medium Zucchini
½ c. Tomato Sauce
½ c. shredded Mozzarella cheese
2 tbsps. Parmesan cheese
Directions:
Set oven to 350 degrees F.
Slice zucchini in half lengthwise and spoon out the core and seeds to form boats.
Place zucchini halves skin side down in a small baking dish.
Add remaining ingredients inside the hollow center then set to bake until golden brown and fork tender (about 30 minutes).
Serve and enjoy.
Nutritional Information:
Calories: 214, Fat: 7.9g, Carbs: 23.6g, Protein: 15.2g

• Pear-Cranberry Pie with Oatmeal Streusel

Preparation Time: 10 minutes
Cooking Time: 1 hour 30 minutes
Servings: 6
Ingredients:
Streusel:
¾ c. oats
1/3 c. stevia
½ tsp. cinnamon
¼ tsp. nutmeg
1 tbsp. cubed butter
Filling:
3 c. cubed pears
2 c. cranberries
½ c. stevia
2½ tbsps. cornstarch
Directions:
Set oven to 350 degrees F.
Combine all streusel ingredients in a food processor and process into a coarse crumb.
Next, combine all filling ingredients in a large bowl and toss to combine.
Transfer filling into pie crust, then top with streusel mix.
Set to bake until golden brown (about an hour). Cool and serve.
Nutritional Information:
Calories: 280, Fat: 9g, Carbs: 47g, Protein: 1g

Dinner

Mixed Sweet Potatoes

Preparation time: 15 min
Cooking time: 1 hr
Servings: 2
Ingredients:
4 medium sweet potatoes, baked
1 tsp. Taco seasoning
1 tsp. Olive oil
1 diced red pepper
½ diced red onion
1 1/3 c. Canned black beans
½ c. Mexican cheese blend
½ c. Greek yogurt
¼ c. Chopped cilantro
½ c. Salsa
Directions:
Mix taco seasoning and yogurt well, then set aside.
Set a skillet over medium heat with oil to get hot.
Add in remaining ingredients, except potatoes, cheese, and salsa, and cook for about 8 min or until fully heated through.
Slightly pierce potatoes down the center and top evenly with all remaining ingredients. Serve.
Nutritional information: Calories 311, Fat 6, Carbs 15, Protein 4, Sodium 155

Asparagus and Parmesan

Preparation time: 10 minutes
Cooking time: 6 minutes
Servings: 1
Ingredients

- 1 tsp. sesame oil
- 11 oz. asparagus
- 1 tsp. chicken stock
- ½ tsp. ground white pepper
- 3 oz. Parmesan

Directions
1. Wash the asparagus and chop it roughly.
2. Sprinkle the chopped asparagus with the chicken stock and ground white pepper.
3. Then sprinkle the vegetables with the sesame oil and shake them.
4. Place the asparagus in the air fryer basket.
5. Cook the vegetables for 4 minutes at 400°F.
6. Meanwhile, shred Parmesan cheese.
7. When the time is over—shake the asparagus gently and sprinkle with the shredded cheese.
8. Cook the asparagus for 2 minutes more at 400°F.
9. After this, transfer the cooked asparagus to the serving plates.
10. Serve and taste it!

Nutrition
- Calories: 189 kcal.
- Fat: 11.6 g.
- Fiber: 3.4 g.
- Carbs: 7.9 g.
- Protein: 17.2 g

Walnut and Cheese Filled Mushrooms

Preparation time: 5 minutes
Cooking time: 10 minutes
Servings: 1
Ingredients

- 4 large Portobello mushroom caps
- ⅓ C. walnuts, minced
- 1 tbsp. canola oil
- ½ C. mozzarella cheese, shredded
- 2 tbsps. fresh parsley, chopped

Directions
1. Preheat the air fryer to 350°F.
2. Grease the air fryer basket with cooking spray.
3. Rub the mushrooms with canola oil and fill them with mozzarella cheese.
4. Top with minced walnuts and arrange on the bottom of the greased air fryer basket.
5. Bake for 10 minutes or until golden on top.

6. Remove, let cool for a few minutes and sprinkle with freshly chopped parsley to serve.

Nutrition
- Calories: 110 kcal.
- Carbs: 6 g.
- Fat: 5 g.
- Protein: 8 g.

Chard With Cheddar

Preparation time: 10 minutes
Cooking time: 11 minutes
Servings: 1
Ingredients

- 3 oz. Cheddar cheese, grated
- 10 oz. Swiss chard
- 3 tbsps. cream
- 1 tbsp. sesame oil
- 1 tsp. salt and pepper to taste

Directions

1. Wash Swiss chard carefully and chop it roughly.
2. After this, sprinkle chopped Swiss chard with salt and ground white pepper.
3. Stir it carefully.
4. Sprinkle Swiss chard with the sesame oil and stir it carefully with the help of 2 spatulas.
5. Preheat the air fryer to 260°F.
6. Put chopped Swiss chard in the air fryer basket and cook for 6 minutes.
7. Shake it after 3 minutes of cooking.
8. Then pour the cream into the air fryer basket and mix it up.
9. Cook the meal for 3 minutes more.
10. Then increase the temperature to 400°F.
11. Sprinkle the meal with the grated cheese and cook for 2 minutes more.
12. After this, transfer the meal to the serving plates. Enjoy!

Nutrition
- Calories: 272 kcal.
- Fat: 22.3 g.
- Fiber: 2.5 g.
- Carbs: 6.7 g.
- Protein: 13.3 g.

Herbed Tomatoes

Preparation time: 10 minutes
Cooking time: 15 minutes
Servings: 1
Ingredients

- 2 big tomatoes, halved and insides scooped out
- 1 tsp. salt and black pepper, to taste
- ½ tbsp. olive oil
- 1 clove garlic, minced
- ¼ tsp. thyme, chopped

Directions

1. In the air fryer, mix tomatoes with thyme, garlic, oil, salt, and pepper.
2. Mix and cook at 390°F for 15 minutes.
3. Serve.

Nutrition
- Calories: 112 kcal.
- Fat: 1 g.
- Carb: 4 g.
- Protein: 4 g.

Cream Potato

Preparation time: 15 minutes
Cooking time: 20 minutes
Servings: 1
Ingredients

- 3 medium potatoes, scrubbed
- ½ tsp. kosher salt
- 1 tbsp. Italian seasoning
- ⅓ C. cream
- ½ tsp. ground black pepper

Directions
1. Slice the potatoes.
2. Preheat the air fryer to 365°F.
3. Make the layer from the sliced potato in the air fryer basket.
4. Sprinkle the potato layer with kosher salt and ground black pepper.
5. After this, make the second layer of the potato and sprinkle it with Italian seasoning.
6. Make the last layer of the sliced potato and pour the cream.
7. Cook the scallop potato for 20 minutes.
8. When the scalloped potato is cooked—let it chill till room temperature. Enjoy!

Nutrition
- Calories: 269 kcal.
- Fat: 4.7 g.
- Fiber: 7.8 g.
- Carbs: 52.6 g.
- Protein: 5.8 g.

Grilled Tomatoes With Black Garlic Spread

Preparation time: 10 minutes
Cooking time: 40 minutes
Servings: 3
Ingredients

- 3 bulbs black garlic (or try white garlic/wild garlic if you can't find black garlic)
- 3 beef tomatoes

Directions
1. Preheat the oven to 350°F.
2. Cut the tops off the black garlic bulbs so that the tops of the cloves are exposed.
3. Place the bulbs on a small ovenproof dish.
4. Slice the beef tomatoes each into four slices and arrange them on an ovenproof dish.
5. Bake the tomatoes and the garlic bulbs in the oven for 35–40 minutes.
6. When done, spread the soft flesh of the garlic on top of the tomato slices to serve.

Nutrition
- Calories: 90 kcal.
- Protein: 6 g.
- Total carbs: 18 g.
- Dietary fiber: 0 g.
- Total fat: 0 g.

Tomato and Arugula Egg White Scramble

Preparation time: 10 minutes
Cooking time: 40 minutes
Servings: 3
Ingredients

- 1 tsp. olive oil cooking spray
- 1 large onion, chopped
- 2 beef tomatoes, diced
- 3 large egg whites, whisked
- 1 C. arugula leaves, shredded

Directions
1. Lightly spray a non-stick pan with the cooking spray, and heat over medium heat.
2. Add the chopped onions, and sauté until they become translucent.
3. Add the diced tomatoes, and cook until the tomatoes have released their liquids, for about three minutes.
4. Add the whisked egg whites and allow them to sit for a couple of minutes.
5. Add the arugula leaves and scramble the egg whites so that the ingredients are well combined.
6. Serve hot.

Nutrition
- Calories: 92 kcal.
- Protein: 10 g.
- Total carbs: 14 g.
- Dietary fiber: 1 g.
- Total fat: 1 g.

Sunshine Pie

Preparation time: 10 minutes
Cooking time: 40 minutes
Servings: 3
Ingredients
- 1 ½ lb. spaghetti squash
- 1 tsp. olive oil
- 1 clove garlic, minced
- 1 tbsp. chopped onions
- ½ C. sliced mushrooms
- ¼ C. chopped red peppers
- 1 C. canned chopped tomatoes
- 1 tsp. dried oregano
- 1 C. Mozzarella cheese, low-fat and shredded

Directions
1. Preheat the oven to 375°F.
2. To prepare the spaghetti squash, half the squash and discard its seeds.
3. Place each half face down in a 9x13-inch baking dish.
4. Cover and bake for 30–40 minutes until soft.
5. Remove and allow to cool.
6. When cool enough to handle, scrape out the squash's flesh and mash to a smooth consistency. Meanwhile, prepare the filling.
7. Heat the olive oil in a large saucepan over medium heat.
8. Add the garlic and onions, and cook for 2 minutes, stirring frequently.
9. Add the mushrooms, bell peppers, chopped tomatoes, and dried oregano to the pan, and bring to a boil.
10. Reduce the heat, and simmer for 15–20 minutes until the sauce has thickened, stirring occasionally.

To assemble:
1. Transfer the tomato filling into an ovenproof serving dish.
2. Top with the squash, and then the Mozzarella cheese.
3. Bake for 25 minutes or until lightly browned.
4. Let cool for 5 minutes before serving.

Nutrition
- Calories: 81 kcal.
- Protein: 6 g.
- Total carbs: 4 g.
- Dietary fiber: 1 g.
- Total fat: 5 g.

Low-Fat Fish Tacos With Kale Leaves

Preparation time: 10 minutes
Cooking time: 40 minutes
Servings: 3
Ingredients

- ¼ C. chopped scallions
- ¼ C. chopped cilantro
- 2 tbsps. fat-free sour cream
- Juice of 1 lime
- ½ clove garlic, minced
- 6 oz. cod, or other white fish fillets, skinless and boneless, cubed
- 1 tsp. ground cumin
- 1 tsp. coriander seeds
- ½ tsp. paprika
- ½ tsp. red pepper flakes
- 2 small whole wheat tortillas
- 1 C. kale leaves, shredded

Directions

1. To make the sauce, combine the chopped scallions, cilantro, sour cream, lime juice, minced garlic in a bowl, and set aside.
2. Season the fish fillet cubes with ground cumin, coriander seeds, paprika, and red pepper flakes.
3. Cook the fish under a hot broiler for 4–5 minutes on each side or until the fish is thoroughly cooked through.
4. Remove and place to one side. When the fish has slightly cooled, mix with the sauce until well combined.
5. Gently toast the tortillas under the broiler for 1–2 minutes.
6. To assemble, spoon the fish onto the tortillas and top with the shredded kale leaves.

Nutrition

- Calories: 227 kcal.
- Protein: 21 g.
- Total carbs: 27 g.
- Dietary fiber: 6 g.

Total fat: 5 g.

Wild Salmon Salad

Preparation time: 10 minutes
Cooking time: 50 minutes
Servings: 3
Ingredients

- 2 medium-sized cucumbers, sliced
- A handful of iceberg lettuce, torn
- ¼ C. sweet corn
- 1 large tomato roughly chopped
- 8 oz. smoked wild salmon, sliced
- 4 tbsps. freshly squeezed orange juice

For the dressing:

- 1 ¼ C. liquid yogurt, 2% fat
- 1 tbsp. fresh mint finely chopped
- 2 garlic cloves, crushed
- 1 tbsp. sesame seeds

Directions

1. Combine vegetables in a large bowl.
2. Drizzle with orange juice and top with salmon slices.
3. Set aside.
4. In another bowl, whisk together yogurt, mint, crushed garlic, and sesame seeds.
5. Drizzle over salad and toss to combine.
6. Serve cold.

Nutrition

- Calories: 249 kcal.
- Protein: 5.6 g.
- Total carbs: 32.8 g.
- Dietary fiber: 3.2 g.

Total fat: 11 g.

Air Fried Spinach Casserole

Preparation time: 15 min
Cooking time: 1 hour
Servings: 2
Ingredients:
¾ c. Unsweetened almond milk
4 eggs
3 oz. Chopped spinach
3 oz. Chopped artichoke hearts

1 c. Grated parmesan
3 minced garlic cloves
1 tsp. Salt
½ tsp. Pepper ¾ c. Coconut flour
1 tbsp. Baking powder

Directions:
Preheat air fryer to 375 degrees f. Grease air fryer pan with cooking time spray. Whisk eggs with almond milk, spinach, artichoke hearts, and ½ cup of parmesan cheese. Add salt, garlic, and pepper. Add the coconut flour and baking powder; whisk until well combined. Spread mixture into air fryer pan and sprinkle remaining cheese over it. Place the baking pan in the air fryer and cook for about 30 min. Remove baking pan from the air fryer and sprinkle with chopped basil. Slice, then serve and enjoy!

Nutritional information: Calories 423, Fat 11, Carbs 43, Protein 12, Sodium 455

- **Fresh Shrimp Spring Rolls V 20**

Preparation Time: 10 minutes
Cooking Time: 20 minutes
Servings: 12
Ingredients:
Rice paper (12 sheets)
Bib lettuce (12 leaves, washed)
Basil (12 leaves, washed)
Cilantro (¾ cup, fresh, washed)
Carrots (1 cup, shredded, washed)
Cucumber (½ medium, thinly sliced)
Shrimp (20oz., cooked, de-veined and peeled)

Directions:
Add all your vegetables, and shrimp to separate bowls and lay out on a flat surface.
Set a damp paper towel tower flat on your work surface.
Quickly wet one of your rice papers under warm water and lay on paper towel.
Top with 1 of each vegetable, and 4 pieces of shrimp, then roll your rice paper into a burrito – like roll.
Repeat until all your vegetables and shrimp has been used up. Serve, and enjoy.

Nutrition:
Calories 67
Total Fat 2.9 g
Total Carbohydrate 7.4 g
Protein 2.6 g

- **Roasted Beet & Arugula**

Preparation Time: 10 minutes
Cooking Time: 25 minutes
Servings: 6
Ingredients:
Beets (2 small, roasted, chopped)
Corn Tortillas (6)
Arugula (1 cup)
Goat cheese (½ cup)
Blackberries (1 cup)
Honey (2 tbsp.)
Balsamic vinegar (2 tbsp.)

Directions:
Set your oven to preheat to 350 F. Lay your tortillas on a flat surface.
Top with beets, berries, and goat cheese. Combine your balsamic vinegar, and honey together in a small bowl, and whisk to combine.
Drizzle the mixture over your pizza, and to bake for about 10 minutes, or until your cheese has melted slightly, and your tortilla crisp.
Garnish with arugula and serve.

Nutrition:
Calories 286
Total Fat 40 g
Total Carbohydrate 42 g
Protein 15 g

Southwestern Black Bean Cakes with Guacamole V

Preparation Time: 10 minutes
Cooking Time: 25 minutes
Servings: 4
Ingredients:
Whole wheat bread crumbs (1 cup)
Cilantro (3 tbsp., fresh, chopped)
Garlic (2 cloves)
Black beans (15 oz. can, low sodium)
Chipotle peppers in Adobo sauce (7 oz. can)
Cumin (1 tsp., ground)
Egg (1 large)
Avocado (½ medium, diced)
Lime juice (1 tbsp.)
Tomato (1 small, plum)
Directions:
Drain beans then add all your ingredients, except avocado, lime juice, and eggs, to a food processor and run until the mixture begin to pull away from the sides of processor.
Transfer to a large bowl and add in egg then mix well.
Form into 4 even patties, and cook on a preheated, greased grill over medium heat for about 10 minutes, flipping halfway through.
Add your avocado, and lime juice in a small bowl, then stir and mash together using a fork.
Season to taste then serve with bean cakes.
Nutrition:
Calories 178
Total Fat 7 g
Total Carbohydrate 25 g
Protein 11 g

Veggie Quesadillas with Cilantro Yogurt Dip V

Preparation Time: 10 minutes
Cooking Time: 25 minutes
Servings: 4
Ingredients:
Black Beans (1 cup)
Cilantro (2 tbsp., chopped)
Bell pepper (½, finely chopped)
Corn kernels (½ cup)
Cheese (1 cup, low-fat, shredded)
Corn tortillas (6, soft)
Carrot (1 medium, shredded)
Directions:
Set your skillet to preheat on low heat. Lay 3 tortillas on a flat surface.
Top evenly with peppers, carrots, cilantro, beans, corn, and cheese over the tortillas (covering each with another tortilla, maximum.
Add your quesadilla to your preheated skillet, and cook until the cheese melts, and tortilla becomes a nice golden brown (about 2 min).
Flip to quesadilla and cook for about a minute (or until golden).
Mix well. Slice each quesadilla into 4 even wedges and serve with your dip. Enjoy!
Nutrition:
Calories 344
Total Fat 8 g
Total Carbohydrate 46 g
Protein 27 g

Mayo-less Tuna Salad 20

Preparation Time: 10 minutes
Cooking Time: 5 minutes
Servings: 2
Ingredients:
Tuna (5 oz., light, in water, drained)
Olive oil (1 tbsp., extra virgin)
Red wine vinegar (1 tbsp.)
Green onion (¼ cup, chopped)
Arugula (2 cups)
Pasta (1 cup, cooked)
Parmesan cheese (1 tbsp., shaved)
Black pepper
Directions:
Combine all your ingredients into a medium bowl.
Split mixture between two plates. Serve, and enjoy.
Nutrition:
Calories 213.2
Total Fat 6.2 g
Total Carbohydrate 20.3 g
Protein 22.7 g

• Southwest Style Zucchini Rice Bowl 20

Preparation Time: 10 minutes
Cooking Time: 12 minutes
Servings: 2
Ingredients:
Vegetable oil (1 tbsp.)
Chopped vegetables (1 cup, of your choice)
Chicken breast (1 cup, grilled, chopped)
Zucchini rice (1 cup, cooked)
Salsa (4 tbsp.)
Cheddar cheese (2 tbsp., shredded)
Sour cream (2 tbsp., low fat)
Directions:
Set a skillet with oil to heat up over medium heat.
Add chopped vegetables and allow to cook, while stirring, until vegetables become fork tender.
Add chicken, and zucchini rice and continue to cook, while stirring, until fully heated through.
Split between 2 serving bowls, and garnish with your remaining ingredients. Serve, and enjoy!
Nutrition:
Calories 168
Total Fat 8.2 g
Total Carbohydrate 18 g
Protein 5.5 g

Pesto & Mozzarella Stuffed Portobello Mushroom Caps V

Preparation Time: 10 minutes
Cooking Time: 30 minutes
Servings: 2
Ingredients:
Mushrooms (2, Portobello caps, cleaned, stems removed)
Tomato (1 small, Roma, diced)
Pesto (2 tbsp.)
Mozzarella cheese (¼ cup, shredded, low-fat)
Directions:
Spoon your pesto into evenly into your mushroom caps, then to with your remaining ingredients.
Set to bake at 400 degrees F for about 15 minutes. Enjoy!
Nutrition:
Calories 112
Total Fat 5.4 g
Total Carbohydrate 7.5 g
Protein 10.5 g

• Pear, Turkey and Cheese Mushroom Sandwich 20

Preparation Time: 10 minutes
Cooking Time: 9 minutes
Servings: 2
Ingredients:
Mushroom (2 halved, portobello)
Mustard (2 tsp., Dijon-style)
Smoked Turkey (2 slices, reduced-sodium)
Pear (1, cored, thinly sliced)
Mozzarella cheese (1/4 cup, shredded, low fat)
Pepper (1/8 tsp., coarsely ground)
Directions:
Use your mustard to spread on both slices of mushrooms, then top each side with turkey and set one side aside.
Top your remaining half with pear slices, and season with pepper.
Close your sandwich, and set to broil for about 3 minutes, or until your cheese has been melted, and turkey warmed. Enjoy!
Nutrition:
Calories 337.3
Total Fat 11.6 g
Total Carbohydrate 55.8 g
Protein 16.5 g

Salmon Salad Pita 20

Preparation Time: 10 minutes
Cooking Time: 5 minutes
Servings: 3
Ingredients:
Salmon (¾ cup, Alaskan)
Yogurt (3 tbsp., plain, fat free)
Lemon juice (1 tbsp.)
Bell pepper (2 tbsp., red, minced)
Red Onion (1 tbsp., minced)
Capers (1 tsp., rinsed, chopped)
Dill (1 tsp, dried)
Lettuce (3 leaves)
Black pepper (to taste)
Pita bread (3 small, whole wheat)
Directions:
In a bowl, create your salmon salad by combining your first 8 ingredients, then stir.
Create salmon pita by spooning your salmon salad evenly onto your letter leaf then placing it inside your pitas. Enjoy!
Nutrition:
Calories 239
Total Fat 7 g
Total Carbohydrate 19 g
Protein 25 g

Thai Tofu Quinoa Bowl

Preparation Time: 10 minutes
Cooking Time: 1 hour 40 minutes
Servings: 8
Ingredients:
2 packages (15 ounces each) extra firm tofu, diced
2 tablespoons sesame oil
3 cups chicken broth
2 cups carrots, shredded
1 cup fresh cilantro
4 tablespoons soy sauce
2 cups uncooked quinoa, rinsed
1 cup almonds, slivered
1 1/3 cups scallions, chopped
For the sauce:
4 teaspoons creamy peanut butter
4 tablespoons rice wine vinegar
1 tablespoon stevia
Juice of a lime
4 tablespoons Sriracha sauce
1/3 cup coconut milk
2 cloves garlic, minced
2 teaspoons ginger, grated
Directions:
Rinse and drain the tofu about 30-40 minutes before cooking.
Wrap with a kitchen towel and place on a rimmed plate. Place something heavy on it like a heavy bottomed pan so that excess moisture in it is pressed out.
Set aside for 15-20 minutes. Chop into pieces.
Place tofu in a bowl. Pour soy sauce and sesame oil on it. Toss well. Transfer the tofu on to a lined baking sheet in a single layer.
Bake in a preheated oven at 350 F for 30-40 minutes or until crisp. Toss frequently while it is baking.
Place a pan over medium heat. Add quinoa and toast it until it turns golden brown. Add broth and stir.
Lower heat and cover with a lid. Simmer until all the broth is absorbed.
Uncover and fluff with a fork. Set aside.
Make the sauce as follows: Add peanut butter to a microwave safe bowl. Microwave on high for 10-12 seconds until it melts.
Remove the bowl from the microwave and add rest of the ingredients of the sauce and whisk well. Set aside.
Nutrition:
Calories 298
Total Fat 22.9 g
Total Carbohydrate 0.4 g
Protein 22.4 g

One-Skillet Peanut Chicken

Preparation Time: 10 minutes
Cooking Time: 30 minutes
Servings: 4
Ingredients:
1-pound chicken breast
2 tablespoons soy sauce
3 tablespoons water
2 cloves garlic, chopped

1 tablespoon ginger paste
2 tablespoons cooking oil
½ cup salsa
2 ½ tablespoons butter
3 green onions, finely chopped
Directions:
Cut chicken breasts horizontally in the shape of cutlets and cut them again in half.
In a bowl add garlic, soy sauce, water, ginger paste. Add this sauce to chicken and toss to combine, let to marinade for 30 minutes.
Meanwhile, combine salsa, and butter. Set aside.
Heat oil in a pan and fry chicken pieces until nicely golden from both sides.
Now add in salsa mixture and cook covered on low till chicken is done.
Garnish green onions and serve with rice.
Nutrition:
Calories 259
Total Fat 4.9g
Total Carbohydrate 12.6g
Protein 42.5g

Turkey Stuffed Zucchini Boats – Italian Style

Preparation Time: 10 minutes
Cooking Time: 2 hours
Servings: 4
Ingredients:
1/4 cup soy sauce
1 tbsp. canola oil
2 tsp sesame oil
1 Tbsp. ginger paste
2 garlic cloves, minced
2 lb. flat iron or flank steak
1/4 cup rice vinegar
1/8 cup stevia
¼ tsp. red pepper flakes
4 cups thinly sliced cabbage
a few green onions, chopped
Directions:
Pre-heat oven to 375F.
Discard the inner portion of zucchini.
Transfer spaghetti sauce in zucchini boats.
Bake for about 15-20 minutes.
Add some cheese if you like and bake again for ten minutes.
Directions for making the sauce:
In a pot add ground turkey and cook for 10-12 minutes.
Heat oil in pan and cook onion with green pepper for 4-5 minutes. Now add in garlic. Cook for another 1-2 minutes by stirring.
Drizzle in wine and cook for about four minutes.
Transfer of crushed tomatoes, a jar of marinara, thyme, paste, stevia, bay leaves, oregano, crushed pepper flakes, and some salt, simmer for few minutes.
Add in cooked meat. Cook covered for 30 minutes.
Enjoy.
Nutrition:
Calories 52
Total Fat 2.9g
Total Carbohydrate 5.6g
Protein 1.1g

Tomato Baked Tilapia with Lemon

Preparation Time: 10 minutes
Cooking Time: 30 minutes
Servings: 4
Ingredients:
4 tilapia fillets
2 tbsp. olive oil
1 tbsp. fresh basil, chopped
1 tbsp. salt
1 large tomato thinly sliced
1 tbsp. lemon zest
Salt & Pepper to taste
¼ teaspoon lime juice
Directions:
Preheat oven to 400F
Brush baking tray with cooking oil.
Spread fish fillets in the tray.
Sprinkle them with salt and pepper.
Now place tomato slices, basil, and garlic on fillets.
Drizzle them with olive oil.
Sprinkle more salt and pepper and drizzle lemon juice.
Bake for about 20 minutes.
Cook on Broil for 5-10 minutes.
Nutrition:
Calories 236
Total Fat 5g
Total Carbohydrate 12g
Protein 18.3g

Stuffed Poblano Peppers 20

Preparation Time: 10 minutes
Cooking Time: 30 minutes
Servings: 4
Ingredients:
Poblano peppers (14, seeded, broiled)
Zucchini rice (½ cup, cooked)
Grilled Salsa (1½ cups, fresh)
Black bean (15 oz., rinsed, drained)
Corn (1½ cup, frozen)
Cumin (1 tsp.)
Chili powder (1 tsp.)
Cayenne pepper (1/8 tsp.)
Pepper (to taste)
Mexican cheese (½ cup, shredded)
Directions:
Add all your ingredients, except peppers, and ½ of your cheese to a large microwave safe bowl, stir and place to warm for about 3 minutes, stopping to stir every 30 seconds.
Spoon your mixture into your peppers and top with remaining cheese.
Set to broil on high until cheese melts (about 3 min). Enjoy!
Nutrition:
Calories 260
Total Fat 6 g
Total Carbohydrate 4g
Protein 20.5 g

Whole Wheat BLT

Preparation Time: 10 minutes
Cooking Time: 4 hours 40 minutes
Servings: 3
Ingredients:
1 package thick-cut Turkey bacon in original vacuum-sealed packaging
6 slices whole wheat bread, toasted
6 slices tomato
3 leaves lettuce
3 tablespoons mayonnaise
Directions:
Preheat the water bath to 140 degrees F. Place sealed Turkey bacon in the water bath.
Cook at least 4 hours or overnight. After at least 4 hours, remove Turkey bacon from pan.
Brown in the hot pan on both sides. Drain on paper towel.
Spread mayonnaise on bread. Assemble sandwiches with tomato and lettuce. Serve.
Nutrition:
Calories 812
Total Fat 70.07g
Total Carbohydrate 22.56g
Protein 22.74g

Massaman Curry Chicken with Sweet Potatoes & Peas

Preparation Time: 10 minutes
Cooking Time: 1 hour
Servings: 4
Ingredients:
6 chicken thighs
2 medium onions, diced
2 sweet potatoes, cubed
1 cup peas
2 cups chicken broth
1 can coconut milk
1 cup water
juice of 1 lime
3 tbsp. Curry Paste
1 tbsp. olive oil
salt and pepper to taste
2 tbsp. cilantro, chopped
2 tbsp. toasted chopped cashews
Directions:
Heat olive oil in a saucepan.
Sprinkle drumsticks with salt and some pepper.
Cook in oil until nicely browned. Remove.
Add the curry paste. Let to cook until smoked.
Now transfer onions and cook for 5 minutes.
Add chicken again to the pan.
Now pour in coconut milk, chicken broth with water.
Now add sweet potatoes with lime and simmer on low flame. Let to cook for 40 minutes.
Garnish with some cilantro.
Sprinkle cashews.
Enjoy!!
Nutrition:
Calories 206
Total Fat 42g
Total Carbohydrate 0.5g Protein 29g

Coconut Adobo Chicken Stuffed Sweet Potatoes

Preparation Time: 10 minutes
Cooking Time: 1 hour 30 minutes
Ingredients:
sweet potatoes (3 large)
chicken breast (3)
Olive Oil (2 tbsp.)
salt and pepper, to taste
bell pepper (1 red, chopped)
green onions (3, chopped)
Coconut Adobo Cooking Sauce (1/2 Jar)
Cilantro (2 Tbsp., chopped)
Roasted cashews (1/4 Cup)
Directions:
Preheat oven to 400 degrees.
Rub sweet potato with olive oil.
Transfer them to the baking sheet and bake for 1 hour.
In a pan heat 1 tbsp. oil and add chicken, salt, and pepper.
Cook for about 5 minutes.
Now add red bell pepper and green onions, cook for another 2-3 minutes.
Add in Adobo Sauce and stir well, cooking for 10 minutes.
Cut sweet potatoes as a half and fill them each with chicken mixture, top with cilantro and some cashews.
Nutrition:
Calories 305
Total Fat 16.1g
Total Carbohydrate 27g
Protein 15.8g

Fennel Quiche V

Preparation Time: 10 minutes
Cooking Time: 33 minutes
Servings: 4
Ingredients:
10 oz. fennel, chopped
1 cup spinach
5 eggs
½ cup almond flour
1 teaspoon olive oil
1 tablespoon butter
1 teaspoon salt
¼ cup heavy cream
1 teaspoon ground black pepper
Directions:
Chop the spinach and combine it with the chopped fennel in the big bowl.
Beat the egg in the separate bowl and whisk them.
Combine the whisked eggs with the almond flour, butter, salt, heavy cream, and ground black pepper. Whisk it.
Preheat the air fryer to 360 F.
Spray the air fryer basket tray with the olive oil inside. Then add the spinach-fennel mixture and pour the whisked egg mixture.
Cook the quiche for 18 minutes. When the time is over – let the quiche chill little. Then remove it from the air fryer and slice into the servings. Enjoy!
Nutrition:
Calories 249
Total Fat 19.1g
Total Carbohydrate 9.4g
Protein 11.3g

Southwest Tortilla Bake V

Preparation Time: 10 minutes
Cooking Time: 1 hour
Servings: 8
Ingredients:
Whole Wheat tortillas (8, cut in half)
Monterey jack cheese (1 cup shredded)
Corn (1 cup, fresh)
Black beans (1 cup, cooked)
Green onions (2, sliced)
Eggs (2)
Milk (1 cup, fat free)
Chili powder (1/2 tsp.)
Green chilies (4 oz., diced)
Tomato (1, sliced)
Salsa
Directions:
Set your oven to preheat oven to 350 degrees F, and lightly grease a square baking dish with oil.
Add 5 tortilla halves onto the bottom of your dish. Top with beans, corn, 1/3 cup of each cheese.
Top evenly with a half of your green onions. Top with another 5 halves of the tortillas, then the remaining vegetables, and another 1/3 cup of cheese.
Finally, top with your remaining 5 tortilla halves.
Add green chilis, milk, chili powder, and eggs then whisk to combine.
Transfer your egg mixture in your baking dish and top with cheese. Set to bake until fully set (about 50 minutes).
Allow to rest for 10 minutes, then top with salsa, and serve.
Nutrition:
Calories 363
Total Fat 15 g
Total Carbohydrate 33 g
Protein 24 g

Cucumber Tuna Salad

Preparation Time: 5 minutes
Cooking Time: 5 minutes
Servings: 6
Ingredients:
2 cans tuna, drained
2/3 cup light mayonnaise
1 cup cucumber, diced
1/2 tsp dried dill
1 tsp fresh lemon juice
Pepper
Salt
Directions:
Add all ingredients into the mixing bowl and mix well.
Serve and enjoy.
Nutrition:
Calories 215

Fat 13.5 g
Carbohydrates 6.9 g
Sugar 2 g
Protein 16.1 g
Cholesterol 25 mg

• Roasted Parmesan Cauliflower

Preparation Time: 10 minutes
Cooking Time: 30 minutes
Servings: 4
Ingredients:
8 cups cauliflower florets
1 tsp Italian seasoning, crushed
2 tbsp olive oil
1/2 cup parmesan cheese, shredded
2 tbsp balsamic vinegar
1/4 tsp pepper
1/4 tsp salt
Directions:
Preheat the oven to 450 F/ 232 C.
Toss cauliflower, Italian seasoning, oil, pepper, and salt in a bowl.
Spread cauliflower on a baking tray and roast for 15-20 minutes.
Toss cauliflower with cheese and vinegar.
Return to the oven and roast for 5-10 minutes more.
Serve and enjoy.
Nutrition:
Calories 196
Fat 13 g
Carbohydrates 12 g
Sugar 4 g
Protein 11 g
Cholesterol 14 mg

• Delicious Chicken Salad

Preparation Time: 10 minutes
Cooking Time: 5 minutes
Servings: 4
Ingredients:
1 lb cooked chicken breasts, diced
1/2 cup olives, sliced
1 tbsp capers
2 tbsp olive oil
2 tbsp vinegar
1/2 cup onion, minced
2 tbsp fresh parsley, chopped
1 tbsp fresh basil, chopped
1/4 tsp chili flakes
Salt
Directions:
Add all ingredients into the mixing bowl and toss well.
Serve and enjoy.
Nutrition:
Calories 315
Fat 18 g
Carbohydrates 3.2 g
Sugar 1 g
Protein 33 g
Cholesterol 100 mg

- **Cauliflower Mushroom Soup**

Preparation Time: 10 minutes
Cooking Time: 26 minutes
Servings: 4
Ingredients:
1 1/2 cup mushrooms, diced
2 cups cauliflower florets
1/2 onion, diced
1 tsp onion powder
1 2/3 cup coconut milk
1/2 tbsp olive oil
1/4 tsp pepper
1/4 tsp salt
Directions:
Add cauliflower, coconut milk, onion powder, pepper, and salt in a saucepan. Bring to boil over medium heat.
Turn heat to low and simmer for 8 minutes.
Puree the soup using an immersion blender until smooth.
Heat oil in another saucepan over high heat.
Add onion and mushrooms and sauté for 8 minutes.
Add cauliflower mixture to sautéed mushrooms. Stir well and bring to boil.
Cover and simmer for 10 minutes.
Serve and enjoy.
Nutrition
Calories 260
Fat 24 g
Carbohydrates 11 g
Sugar 5 g
Protein 4 g
Cholesterol 0 mg

- **Cauliflower Broth**

Preparation Time: 10 minutes
Cooking Time: 20 minutes
Servings: 4
Ingredients:
1/2 head cauliflower, diced
1 small onion, diced
1 tbsp olive oil
1 garlic clove, minced
15 oz vegetable broth
1/2 tsp salt
Directions:
Heat olive oil in a saucepan over medium heat.
Add onion and garlic and sauté for 5 minutes.
Add cauliflower and broth. Stir well and bring to boil.
Cover and simmer for 15 minutes. Season with salt.
Puree the soup using an immersion blender until smooth.
Serve and enjoy.
Nutrition:
Calories 41
Fat 1.5 g
Carbohydrates 4.1 g
Sugar 2 g
Protein 3.2 g
Cholesterol 0 mg

- **Cauliflower Mash**

Preparation Time: 10 minutes
Cooking Time: 10 minutes
Servings: 4
Ingredients:
1 lb cauliflower, cut into florets
1/2 lemon juice
3 oz parmesan cheese, grated
4 oz butter
Pepper
Salt
Directions:
Boil cauliflower florets in the salted water until tender. Drain well.
Transfer cauliflower into the blender with remaining ingredients and blend until smooth.
Serve and enjoy.
Nutrition:
Calories 300
Fat 27 g
Carbohydrates 7 g
Sugar 3 g
Protein 9 g
Cholesterol 75 mg

- **Curried Egg Salad**

Preparation Time: 5 minutes
Cooking Time: 5 minutes

Servings: 4
Ingredients:
6 hard-boiled eggs, peel and chop
1/2 cup light mayonnaise
1 tsp curry powder
Directions:
Add all ingredients into the mixing bowl and mix well.
Serve and enjoy.
Nutrition:
Calories 210
Fat 15 g
Carbohydrates 7 g
Sugar 2 g
Protein 8 g
Cholesterol 250 mg

• Dijon Potato Salad

Preparation Time: 10 minutes
Cooking Time: 20 minutes
Servings: 5
Ingredients:
1 lb potatoes
1/2 lime juice
2 tbsp olive oil
2 tbsp fresh dill, chopped
2 tbsp chives, minced
1/2 tbsp vinegar
1 tbsp Dijon mustard
1/2 lime zest
Pepper
Salt
Directions:
Add water in a large pot and bring to boil.
Add potatoes in boiling water and cook for 15 minutes or until tender. Drain well and set aside.
In a small bowl, whisk together vinegar, mustard, lime zest, lime juice, olive oil, dill, and chives.
Peel potatoes and diced and transfer in mixing bowl.
Pour vinegar mixture over potatoes and stir to coat.
Season with pepper and salt.
Serve and enjoy.
Nutrition:
Calories 115
Fat 6 g
Carbohydrates 15 g
Sugar 1 g
Protein 2 g
Cholesterol 0 mg

• Carrot Sweet Potato Soup

Preparation Time: 10 minutes
Cooking Time: 8 minutes
Servings: 4
Ingredients:
1 lb sweet potato, peeled and cut into chunks
1/2 lb carrots, chopped
1 tbsp olive oil
1 tbsp ginger, grated
6 cups vegetable broth
Pepper
Salt
Directions:
Heat oil in a saucepan over medium heat.
Add carrots and sweet potato and sauté for 10 minutes.
Add ginger and cook for 2 minutes.
Add broth and stir well. Bring to boil.
Turn heat to low and simmer for 20 minutes.
Remove pan from heat. Puree the soup using an immersion blender until smooth.
Season with pepper and salt.
Serve and enjoy.
Nutrition:
Calories 218
Fat 5.8 g
Carbohydrates 31.4 g
Sugar 11.2 g
Protein 10.1 g
Cholesterol 0 mg

Creamy Salmon Salad

Preparation Time: 10 minutes
Cooking Time: 5 minutes
Servings: 2
Ingredients:
6 oz can salmon, drained
1 celery stalk, sliced
1 avocado, chopped
1/2 bell pepper, chopped
2 tbsp low-fat yogurt
2 tbsp mustard
1/4 cup onion, minced
Directions:
In a mixing bowl, whisk together yogurt and mustard. Add remaining ingredients and stir to combine.
Serve and enjoy.
Nutrition:
Calories 405
Fat 27.8 g
Carbohydrates 17.5 g
Sugar 4.6 g
Protein 24.3 g
Cholesterol 34 mg

Baked Dijon Salmon

Preparation Time: 10 minutes
Cooking Time: 10 minutes
Servings: 6
Ingredients:
1 lb salmon
3 tbsp olive oil
1 tsp ginger, grated
2 tbsp Dijon mustard
1 tsp pepper
Salt
Directions:
In a small bowl, mix together oil, mustard, ginger, and pepper.
Preheat the oven to 400 F/ 200 C.
Spray a baking tray with cooking spray and set aside.
Place salmon on a baking tray and spread oil mixture over salmon evenly.
Bake salmon for 10 minutes.
Serve and enjoy.

Nutrition:
Calories 165
Fat 11.9 g
Carbohydrates 0.7 g
Sugar 0.1 g
Protein 15 g
Cholesterol 33 mg

Dijon Chicken Thighs

Preparation Time: 5 minutes
Cooking Time: 50 minutes
Servings: 4
Ingredients:
1 1/2 lbs chicken thighs, skinless and boneless
2 tbsp Dijon mustard
1/4 cup French mustard
2 tsp olive oil
Directions:
Preheat the oven to 375 F/ 190 C.
In a mixing bowl, mix together olive oil, Dijon mustard, and French mustard.
Add chicken to the bowl and mix until chicken is well coated.
Arrange chicken in a baking dish and bake for 45-50 minutes.
Serve and enjoy.
Nutrition:
Calories 348
Fat 15.2 g
Carbohydrates 0.4 g
Sugar 0.1 g
Protein 49.6 g
Cholesterol 151 mg

Herb Pork Chops

Preparation Time: 10 minutes
Cooking Time: 1 hour 15 minutes
Servings: 4
Ingredients:
4 pork chops, boneless
1/2 tsp dried sage
1/2 tsp dried parsley
2 tsp chives
1/2 cup chicken broth

1 tbsp butter
1 tbsp olive oil
1/4 tsp pepper
1/4 tsp salt
Directions:
Preheat the oven to 350 F/ 180 C.
Spray a baking dish with cooking spray and set aside.
Season pork chops with pepper and salt and place in prepared dish.
In a small bowl, mix together butter, oil, sage, parsley, and chives.
Rub butter mixture on top of each pork chops.
Add broth in the baking dish around the pork chops.
Cover with foil and bake for 1 hour.
Remove cover and bake for 15 minutes more.
Serve and enjoy.
Nutrition:
Calories 317
Fat 26.4 g
Carbohydrates 0.3 g
Sugar 0.1 g
Protein 18.7 g
Cholesterol 76 mg

• Taco Chicken

Preparation Time: 5 minutes
Cooking Time: 6 hours
Servings: 4
Ingredients:
1 lb chicken breasts, skinless and boneless
2 tbsp taco seasoning
1 cup chicken broth
Directions:
Place chicken in the slow cooker.
Mix together chicken broth and taco seasoning and pour over chicken.
Cover and cook on low for 6 hours.
Shred chicken using a fork.
Serve and enjoy.
Nutrition:
Calories 233
Fat 8.7 g
Carbohydrates 1.7 g
Sugar 0.5 g
Protein 34 g
Cholesterol 101 mg

• Broiled Fish Fillet

Preparation Time: 5 minutes
Cooking Time: 10 minutes
Servings: 2
Ingredients:
2 cod fish fillets
1/8 tsp curry powder
2 tsp butter
1/4 tsp paprika
1/8 tsp pepper
1/8 tsp salt
Directions:
Preheat the broiler.
Spray broiler pan with cooking spray and set aside.
In a small bowl, mix together paprika, curry powder, pepper, and salt.
Coat fish fillet with paprika mixture and place on broiler pan.
Broil fish for 10-12 minutes.
Top with butter and serve.
Nutrition:
Calories 224
Fat 5.4 g
Carbohydrates 0.3 g
Sugar 0 g
Protein 41.2 g
Cholesterol 109 mg

Chicken Skewers

Preparation Time: 5 minutes
Cooking Time: 10 minutes
Servings: 2
Ingredients:
1 lb chicken breasts, skinless, boneless and cut into cubes
2 tbsp fresh lemon juice
1 tbsp fresh oregano, chopped
2 tbsp olive oil
1/8 tsp cayenne pepper
Pepper
Salt
Directions:
Place chicken in a bowl.
Add reaming ingredients over chicken and mix well.
Place chicken in the refrigerator for 1 hour.
Heat grill over medium heat.
Spray grill with cooking spray.
Thread marinated chicken onto skewers.
Arrange skewers on grill and grill until chicken is cooked.
Serve and enjoy.
Nutrition:
Calories 560
Fat 31 g
Carbohydrates 1.8 g
Sugar 0.4 g
Protein 66 g
Cholesterol 200 mg

Grilled Chicken Breasts

Preparation Time: 10 minutes
Cooking Time: 15 minutes
Servings: 4
Ingredients:
2 lbs chicken breasts, halves
6 tbsp fresh parsley, minced
6 tbsp olive oil
1 1/2 tsp dried oregano
1 tsp paprika
1 tbsp garlic, minced
6 tbsp fresh lemon juice
Pepper
Salt
Directions:
Pierce chicken breasts using a fork. Season with pepper and salt.
Add lemon juice, oregano, paprika, garlic, parsley, and olive oil into the zip-lock bag.
Add chicken to the zip-lock bag.
Seal bag and shake well and place in the refrigerator for 1-2 hours.
Heat grill over medium-high heat.
Place marinated chicken on the grill and cook for 5-6 minutes on each side.
Serve and enjoy.
Nutrition:
Calories 625
Fat 38 g
Carbohydrates 2 g
Sugar 0.6 g
Protein 65 g
Cholesterol 200 mg

Chili Garlic Salmon

Preparation Time: 5 minutes
Cooking Time: 2 minutes
Servings: 3
Ingredients:
1 lb salmon fillet, cut into three pieces
1 tsp red chili powder
1 garlic clove, minced
1 tsp ground cumin
Pepper
Salt
Directions:
Pour 1 1/2 cups water into the instant pot and place trivet into the pot.
In a small bowl, mix together chili powder, garlic, cumin, pepper, and salt.
Rub salmon pieces with spice mixture and place on top of the trivet.
Seal the instant pot with a lid and cook on steam mode for 2 minutes.
Once done, release pressure using the quick-release method than open the lid.
Serve and enjoy.
Nutrition:

Calories 205
Fat 9 g
Carbohydrates 1.1 g
Sugar 0.1 g
Protein 30 g
Cholesterol 65 mg

•Baked Lemon Tilapia

Preparation Time: 10 minutes
Cooking Time: 12 minutes
Servings: 4
Ingredients:
4 tilapia fillets
2 tbsp fresh lemon juice
1 tsp garlic, minced
1/4 cup olive oil
2 tbsp fresh parsley, chopped
1 lemon zest
Pepper
Salt
Directions:
Preheat the oven to 425 F/ 220 C.
Spray a baking dish with cooking spray and set aside.
In a small bowl, whisk together olive oil, lemon zest, lemon juice, and garlic.
Season fish fillets with pepper and salt and place in the baking dish.
Pour olive oil mixture over fish fillets.
Bake fish fillets in the oven for 10-12 minutes.
Garnish with parsley and serve.
Nutrition:
Calories 252
Fat 14.7 g
Carbohydrates 0.5 g
Sugar 0.2 g
Protein 32.2 g
Cholesterol 85 mg

Dessert and Snacks

Garlic Bread

Preparation Time: 5 minutes
Cooking Time: 5 minutes
Servings: 2
Ingredients:
½ cup butter, melted
Pinch salt
1 tablespoon fresh parsley, chopped
4 cloves garlic, roasted and minced
1 loaf French bread, sliced in half lengthwise
Directions:
Mix the butter, salt, parsley and garlic in a bowl.
Spread mixture on top of French bread.
Air fry at 400 degrees F for 3 minutes.
Let cool for 2 minutes before serving.
Nutrition: Calories 312, Fat 6, Carbs 18, Protein 9, Sodium 385

Chocolate Soufflé

Preparation time: 7 minutes
Cooking time: 12 minutes
Servings: 1
Ingredients

- 2 tbsps. almond flour
- ½ tsp. vanilla
- 3 tbsps. sweetener
- 2 separated eggs
- ¼ C. melted coconut oil
- 2 oz. semi-sweet chocolate, chopped

Directions
1. Preheat the Smart Air Fryer Oven to 330°F.
2. Brush coconut oil and sweetener onto ramekins.
3. Melt coconut oil and chocolate together.
4. Beat egg yolks well, adding vanilla and sweetener.
5. Stir in flour and ensure there are no lumps.
6. Whisk egg whites till they reach peak state and fold them into chocolate mixture.
7. Pour batter into ramekins and place into the Smart Air Fryer Oven, then cook for 12 minutes.
8. Serve with powdered sugar dusted on top.
Nutrition
- Calories: 378 kcal.
- Fat 9 g.
- Carbs: 5 g.
- Protein: 4 g.

Cream Cheese Wontons

Preparation time: 5 minutes
Cooking time: 5 minutes
Servings: 1
Ingredients

- 1 egg mixed with a bit of water
- Wonton wrappers
- ½ C. powdered Erythritol
- Softened cream cheese
- Olive oil

Directions
1. Mix sweetener and cream cheese together.
2. Lay out four wontons at a time and cover with a dish towel to prevent drying out.
3. Place ½ tsp. cream cheese mixture into each wrapper.
4. Dip finger into egg/water mixture and fold diagonally to form a triangle.
5. Seal the edges well and repeat with the remaining ingredients.
6. Place filled wontons into the Smart Air Fryer Oven and cook 5 minutes at 400°F, shaking halfway through cooking.
Nutrition
- Calories: 378 kcal.
- Fat: 9 g.
- Carbs: 5 g.
- Protein: 4 g.

Angel Food Cake

Preparation time: 5 minutes
Cooking time: 30 minutes
Servings: 1
Ingredients

- ¼ C. butter, melted
- 1 C. powdered Erythritol
- 1 tsp. strawberry extract
- 12 egg whites
- 2 tsps. cream of tartar

Directions

1. Preheat the air fryer oven for 5 minutes.
2. Blend the cream of tartar and egg whites.
3. Use a hand mixer and whisk until white and fluffy.
4. Add the rest of the ingredients except for the butter and whisk for another minute.
5. Pour into a baking dish.
6. Place in the air fryer basket and cook for 30 minutes at 400°F or if a toothpick inserted in the middle comes out clean.
7. Drizzle with melted butter once cooled.

Nutrition

- Calories: 65 kcal.
- Protein: 3.1 g.
- Fat: 5 g.
- Carbs: 6.2 g.

Chocolate Brownies With Almond Butter

Preparation time: 10 minutes
Cooking time: 40 minutes
Servings: 3
Ingredients

- Nonstick cooking spray
- ½ C. cocoa powder
- 1 tbsp. ground flaxseed
- ½ tsp. ground instant coffee
- ¼ tsp. baking soda
- ½ C. agave nectar
- ½ C. almond butter
- 2 large eggs
- ¼ C. melted coconut oil
- 1 tsp. vanilla extract

Directions

1. Preheat the oven to 325°F.
2. Coat an 8 by 8-inch glass baking dish with the cooking spray.
3. Place the cocoa powder, flaxseed, instant coffee, baking soda, almond butter, coconut oil, eggs, vanilla extract, agave nectar in a high-speed blender or food processor.
4. Blend on medium-high until smooth.
5. Pour the batter into the baking dish.
6. Bake for 25 minutes or until a toothpick inserted in the middle comes out clean.
7. Let cool for 10 minutes before cutting into 16 squares.

Nutrition

- Calories: 124 kcal.
- Protein: 3 g.
- Total carbs: 11 g.
- Dietary fiber: 2 g.

Total fat: 9 g.

Lemon Blackberry Frozen Yogurt

Preparation time: 10 minutes
Cooking time: 30 minutes
Servings: 3

Ingredients

- 4 C. frozen blackberries
- ½ C. low-fat Greek yogurt
- Juice of 1 lemon
- 2 tsps. liquid stevia
- Fresh mint leaves, for garnish

Directions

1. In a blender or a food processor, add the blackberries, yogurt, lemon juice, and stevia.
2. Blend until smooth for about 5 minutes.
3. Serve immediately or freeze in an airtight container and use within 3 weeks.
4. Garnish with fresh mint leaves.

Nutrition

- Calories: 68 kcal.
- Protein: 3 g.
- Total carbs: 15 g.
- Dietary fiber: 5 g.
- Total fat: 0 g.

Low-Calorie Cherry Chocolate Ice Cream

Preparation time: 10 minutes
Cooking time: 20 minutes
Servings: 3

Ingredients

- 2 C. cherries, fresh
- ½ banana
- ½ C. unsweetened almond milk
- 3 tbsps. dairy-free chocolate chips

Directions

1. Wash and dry the cherries, and remove all the pits.
2. Place in a freezer bag or glass container, and freeze for at least three hours. If you don't have the time, you can use frozen cherries.
3. Peel a banana, and place half in the freezer.
4. Pour ¼ C. of the almond milk into ice cube trays (save the other ¼ C.), and freeze those as well, for at least three hours.
5. Place the frozen cherries, half a frozen banana, ice cubes, and ¼ C. of almond milk in a food processor, and process until completely smooth, several minutes.
6. Stir in chocolate chips, and enjoy immediately!

Nutrition

- Calories: 126 kcal.
- Protein: 2.1 g.
- Total carbs: 22.3 g.
- Dietary fiber: 2.8 g.
- Total fat: 4 g.

Skinny Mug Brownie

Preparation time: 10 minutes
Cooking time: 30 minutes
Servings: 3

Ingredients

- 1 tbsp. cocoa powder, unsweetened
- 2 packets Truvia (may be substituted for other sweeteners)
- 2 tbsps. all-purpose flour (may be substituted for almond flour)
- 3 tbsps. almond milk (may be substituted for regular milk or yogurt)

Directions

1. Place all ingredients in a microwave-safe mug.
2. Mix with a fork or small whisk.
3. Microwave on high for 60 seconds.
4. Enjoy.

Nutrition

- Calories: 97 kcal.
- Protein: 1.2 g.
- Total carbs: 9.2 g.
- Dietary fiber: 2.2 g.
- Total fat: 2.2 g.

Carrot Cake

Preparation time: 10 minutes
Cooking time: 30 minutes
Servings: 3

Ingredients

- ¼ C. flour
- Just over ½ tsp. cinnamon
- ¼ tsp. baking powder
- 1/8 tsp. baking soda
- ⅓ C. canned carrots, drained
- 1/8 tsp. salt
- 1 ½ tbsp. brown sugar
- Pinch of uncut Stevia
- 1 tbsp. sugar
- 1 tbsp. milk of choice
- Optional: ½ tsp. ginger or 2 tsp. flax meal
- 1 tbsp. oil, or more milk of choice
- ¼ tsp. pure vanilla extract

Directions

1. In a small bowl, mix dry ingredients (not carrots).
2. If you have a blender or Magic Bullet, mix all wet ingredients and blend.
3. Mix dry mixture into the wet mixture, and stir.
4. Pour this mixture into a greased little dish.
5. In the case of the microwave, cook for 1 minute 20 seconds. Or cook in the oven at 350°F for around 15 minutes.
6. Let cool before trying to pop out.

Nutrition

- Calories: 70 kcal.
- Protein: 2.5 g.
- Total carbs: 17 g.
- Dietary fiber: 3 g.
- Total fat: 0.5 g.

Mini Plum Cakes

Preparation time: 10 minutes
Cooking time: 50 minutes
Servings: 3

Ingredients

- ¾ C. all-purpose flour
- ¼ flaxseed meal
- 1 ½ tsps. baking powder
- ¼ tsp. kosher salt
- 3 tbsps. unsalted butter, at room temperature
- 2 tbsps. avocado
- ⅓ C. sugar
- 1 large egg
- ⅔ C. low-fat milk
- 1 tsp. finely grated lemon zest
- 1 tsp. vanilla extract
- 1 plum, or any stone fruit, pitted and cut into thin slices
- 2 tbsps. raw sugar (optional)

Directions

1. Preheat the oven to 350°F.
2. Use nonstick spray to coat the muffin pan.
3. Whisk baking powder, flaxseed meal, flour, and salt in a bowl.
4. Put aside. Use an electric processor to beat avocado, butter, and sugar in another bowl until light and fluffy, about 2 minutes.
5. Add egg, lemon zest, and vanilla and beat until combined. With the mixer on low speed, add dry ingredients in 3 additions alternating with milk in 2 additions, beginning and ending with dry ingredients.
6. Pour batter evenly among muffin cups.
7. Sprinkle plum slices and raw sugar on top.
8. Bake for 20–25 minutes until golden.
9. Transfer pan to a wire rack; let pan cool for 5 minutes.
10. Transfer cakes to rack and let cool completely.

Nutrition

- Calories: 113 kcal.
- Protein: 3 g.
- Total carbs: 14 g.
- Dietary fiber: 1 g.
- Total fat: 5 g.

Lemonade Cupcakes

Preparation time: 10 minutes
Cooking time: 30 minutes
Servings: 3

Ingredients

- 1 (15.25 oz.) box of white cake mix
- 1 C. water
- ⅓ C. unsweetened applesauce
- 1 tbsp. lemon zest
- 1 ½ tbsps. sugar-free lemonade mix
- 1 (8 oz.) tub of light whipped topping

Directions
1. Preheat oven to 350°F.
2. Line muffin cups with liners (paper).
3. In a medium mixing bowl, combine water, cake mix, lemon zest, applesauce, and 1 tbsp of the sugar-free lemonade mix.
4. Spoon batter evenly into cupcake cups.
5. Bake until a toothpick inserted into the center comes out clean, about 17 minutes.
6. Transfer cupcakes immediately to a rack to cool. While cupcakes are cooling, make the frosting by combining the whipped topping and the remaining ½ tbsp. sugar-free lemonade mix.
7. Once cupcakes are completely cool, top with frosting and serve.

Nutrition

- Calories: 100 kcal.
- Protein: 0.8 g.
- Total carbs: 16.7 g.
- Dietary fiber: 0.2 g.
- Total fat: 3 g.

Mozzarella Bites

Preparation Time: 5 minutes
Cooking Time: 5 minutes
Servings: 4
Ingredients:
8 mozzarella sticks
2 tablespoons butter
¼ breadcrumbs
Directions:
Dip the mozzarella sticks in butter.
Dredge with breadcrumbs.
Arrange in the air fryer basket.
Cook at 320 degrees F for 5 minutes, stirring once.
Nutrition: Calories 312, Fat 6, Carbs 18, Protein 9, Sodium 385

Ranch Pretzels

Preparation Time: 5 minutes
Cooking Time: 5 minutes
Servings: 4
Ingredients:
10 oz. pretzels
2 tablespoons olive oil
1 packet dry ranch seasoning mix
Directions:
Coat the pretzels with olive oil.
Sprinkle all sides with ranch seasoning.
Arrange the pretzels in the air fryer basket.
Cook at 320 degrees F for 3 minutes.
Turn and cook for another 2 minutes.
Nutrition: Calories 312, Fat 6, Carbs 18, Protein 9, Sodium 385

Maple Barbecue Cashews

Preparation Time: 5 minutes
Cooking Time: 5 minutes
Servings: 12
Ingredients:
2 tablespoons olive oil
2 teaspoons maple barbecue rub
1 cup raw cashews
Directions:
Blend olive oil and maple barbecue rub.
Coat cashews with this mixture.
Add to the air fryer basket.
Air fry at 370 degrees F for 5 minutes, stirring once.
Nutrition: Calories 312, Fat 6, Carbs 18, Protein 9, Sodium 385

Pizza Bread

Preparation Time: 10 minutes

Cooking Time: 5 minutes
Servings: 4
Ingredients:
1 cup marinara sauce
2 French bread, sliced in half lengthwise
½ cup mozzarella sauce, shredded
1 tablespoon fresh parsley, chopped
1 tablespoon fresh oregano, chopped
Directions:
Spread marina sauce on top of bread.
Sprinkle the mozzarella cheese on top.
Add the chopped herbs on top.
Air fry at 400 degrees F for 5 minutes.
Nutrition: Calories 312, Fat 6, Carbs 18, Protein 9, Sodium 385

• Mexican Corn

Preparation Time: 5 minutes
Cooking Time: 10 minutes
Servings: 4
Ingredients:
4 ears corn
¼ cup Cotija cheese, crumbled
¼ cup fresh cilantro, chopped
¼ teaspoon chili powder
Directions:
Add the corn to the air fryer basket.
Air fry at 390 degrees F for 10 minutes.
Sprinkle with the Cotija cheese.
Cook for 5 more minutes.
Sprinkle with the cilantro and chili powder.
Nutrition: Calories 312, Fat 6, Carbs 18, Protein 9, Sodium 385

• Smoky Chickpeas

Preparation Time: 5 minutes
Cooking Time: 18 minutes
Servings: 4
Ingredients:
15 oz. chickpeas, rinsed and drained
1 tablespoon sunflower oil
Salt to taste
2 tablespoons lemon juice
½ teaspoon ground cumin
¾ teaspoon smoked paprika
½ teaspoon granulated garlic
Directions:
Preheat your air fryer to 390 degrees F.
Cook chickpeas for 15 minutes, shaking the basket once.
In a bowl, mix the oil, salt, lemon juice and spices.
Toss the chickpeas in the spice mixture.
Air fry at 360 degrees F for 3 minutes.
Nutrition: Calories 312, Fat 6, Carbs 18, Protein 9, Sodium 385

• Potato Chips

Preparation Time: 5 minutes
Cooking Time: 15 minutes
Servings: 4
Ingredients:
Cooking spray
1 potato, sliced thinly
Salt to taste
Directions:
Spray your air fryer basket with oil.
Spray the potato slices with oil.
Sprinkle potato with salt.
Air fry at 450 degrees F for 15 minutes, stirring once or twice.
Nutrition: Calories 312, Fat 6, Carbs 18, Protein 9, Sodium 385

• Roasted Macadamia

Preparation Time: 5 minutes
Cooking Time: 10 minutes
Servings: 4
Ingredients:
1 lb. macadamia nuts
Salt to taste
Directions:
Spread the macadamia nuts in the air fryer basket.
Cook at 250 degrees F for 10 minutes, shaking the basket halfway through.
Sprinkle with salt.
Nutrition: Calories 312, Fat 6, Carbs 18, Protein 9, Sodium 385

Apricot Brie Snack

Preparation Time: 10 minutes
Cooking Time: 5 minutes
Servings: 8
Ingredients:
1 package crescent dough sheets
4 oz. brie cheese, sliced
½ cup apricot preserves
Directions:
Spread the crescent dough sheet on your kitchen table.
Press the sheet onto muffin cups.
Top with the cheese and apricot preserves.
Air fry at 340 degrees F for 5 minutes.
Nutrition: Calories 312, Fat 6, Carbs 18, Protein 9, Sodium 385

Garlic-Parmesan Cheesy Chips

Preparation Time: 2 mimutes
Cooking Time: 27 minutes
Servings: 12
Ingredients:
¼ cup shredded Parmesan cheese
¼ cup shredded sharp Cheddar cheese
¼ teaspoon garlic powder
Dash salt
Directions:
Preheat the oven to 400°F. Line a large baking sheet with parchment paper.
In a medium mixing bowl, combine the Parmesan cheese, Cheddar cheese, garlic powder, and salt. Mix well.
Place 2 teaspoons of the cheese mixture about an inch or two apart on the baking sheet, making about 12 chips.
Bake for 5 to 7 minutes, or until the chips are golden brown around the edges.
Remove from the oven and let sit for 15 to 20 minutes, or until the chips start to crisp. Enjoy.
Nutrition: (6 CHIPS): Calories: 98; Protein: 8g; Fat: 7g; Carbohydrate: 1g; Fiber: 0g; Sugar: 0g; Sodium: 333mg

Cheesy Baked Radish Chips

Preparation Time: 5 minutes
Cooking Time: 40 minutes
Serving: 1
Ingredients:
1 cup thinly sliced radishes (2 bunches radishes)
1 tablespoon extra-virgin olive oil
3 tablespoons nutritional yeast flakes
¼ teaspoon salt
Dash freshly ground black pepper (optional)
Directions:
Preheat the oven to 375°F. Line a baking sheet with parchment paper.
Place the radishes into a small bowl and toss in the oil.
In a small cup, mix the nutritional yeast, salt, and pepper (if using).
Place the oil-coated radish slices onto the prepared baking sheet in a single layer and sprinkle the nutritional yeast mixture lightly onto each slice.
Bake for about 15 minutes, then flip the chips and bake for another 15 minutes. Remove crispy chips, then continue to bake any remaining chips for a few minutes more at a time, until crispy and golden brown.
Serve and enjoy alone or with your favorite low-carbohydrate dip.
Nutrition: (½ CUP CHIPS): Calories: 99; Protein: 5g; Fat: 7g; Carbohydrates: 4g; Fiber: 2g; Sugar: 0g; Sodium: 313mg

Savory Cheese Biscuits

Preparation Time: 5 minutes
Cooking Time: 15 minutes
Servings: 8
Ingredients:
1 cup almond flour
¼ cup shredded Parmesan cheese
¼ cup shredded Cheddar cheese
2 teaspoons baking powder
2 teaspoons garlic powder
½ teaspoon salt
2 large eggs
Directions:
Preheat the oven to 350°F. Line a large baking sheet with parchment paper and set aside.
In a large bowl, add the almond flour, Parmesan cheese, Cheddar cheese, baking powder, garlic powder, and salt. Mix well. Add the eggs and combine.
Scoop a heaping tablespoon of the mixture onto the baking sheet. Using a spatula, flatten the batter slightly

into about 2-inch circles. Repeat, placing biscuits about an inch apart. This should yield 8 small biscuits.

Bake for 15 minutes, or until the top of biscuits is slightly golden brown. Serve warm.

Nutrition: (2 BISCUITS): Calories: 275; Protein: 15g; Fat: 23g; Carbohydrates: 8g; Fiber: 3g; Sugar: 1g; Sodium: 447mg

Italian Herb Muffins

Preparation Time: 5 minutes
Cooking Time: 12 minutes
Servings: 4
Ingredients:
Nonstick cooking spray
8 tablespoons almond flour
¼ cup shredded Parmesan cheese
1 large egg
1 teaspoon garlic powder
1 teaspoon Italian seasoning
1 teaspoon baking powder
¼ teaspoon salt
Directions:

Preheat the oven to 350°F. Line a muffin pan with 4 cupcake liners and spray the liners with nonstick cooking spray.

In a large mixing bowl, combine the almond flour, Parmesan cheese, egg, garlic powder, Italian seasoning, baking powder, and salt. Mix well until fully incorporated.

Scoop heaping tablespoons of the mixture into the lined cups until all the batter is used.

Bake for 12 minutes or until golden brown on the tops. Enjoy warm.

Nutrition: (1 MUFFIN): Calories: 128; Protein: 7g; Fat: 10g; Carbohydrates: 5g; Fiber: 2g; Sugar: 1g; Sodium: 217mg

Cheesy Cauliflower Tots

Preparation Time: 5 minutes
Cooking Time: 15 minutes
Servings: 4
Ingredients:
1 cup cauliflower rice
½ cup almond flour
½ cup shredded mozzarella cheese
1 large egg
1 tablespoon cornstarch
¼ teaspoon salt
Directions:

Preheat the oven to 400°F. Line a large baking sheet with parchment paper and set aside.

In a large mixing bowl, combine the cauliflower rice, almond flour, mozzarella cheese, egg, cornstarch, and salt. Mix well until fully incorporated.

Scoop heaping tablespoons of the mixture onto the baking sheet about an inch apart until all the batter is used. This recipe should make about 16 tots.

Bake for 13 to 15 minutes, until crispy and golden brown. Serve and enjoy.

Nutrition: (4 TOTS): Calories: 152; Protein: 9g; Fat: 11g; Carbohydrates: 6g; Fiber: 2g; Sugar: 1g; Sodium: 253mg

Mozzarella Mushroom Caps

Preparation Time: 5 minutes
Cooking Time: 20 minutes
Servings: 12
Ingredients:
12 white mushroom caps
4 ounces fresh mozzarella pearls
2 tablespoons almond flour
1 tablespoon whipped butter
½ teaspoon garlic powder
Dash salt
Directions:

Preheat the oven to 350°F. Line a baking sheet with parchment paper.

Wash the mushrooms and carefully remove the cap from each one. Place the mushrooms onto the lined baking sheet.

Place about three mozzarella pearls (about 1 tablespoon) in each mushroom cap.

In a small bowl, mix the almond flour, whipped butter, garlic powder, and salt. Sprinkle the mixture on top of each mushroom cap.

Bake for about 20 minutes or until the cheese has melted. Enjoy warm.

Nutrition: (3 MUSHROOM CAPS): Calories: 117; Protein: 8g; Fat: 9g; Carbohydrates: 4g; Fiber: 1g; Sugar: 0.25g; Sodium: 141mg

Almond-Crusted Mozzarella Sticks

Preparation Time: 10 minutes
Cooking Time: 6 minutes
Servings: 6
Ingredients:
1 tablespoon cornstarch
8 tablespoons almond flour
½ teaspoon Italian seasoning
¼ teaspoon salt
2 large eggs
6 (1-ounce) light mozzarella sticks
1 tablespoon extra-virgin olive oil
Directions:

Place the cornstarch on a small plate. On a separate small plate, mix the almond flour, Italian seasoning, and salt. Beat the eggs in a small bowl and place between the two plates.

Cut the mozzarella sticks in half. Lightly coat each mozzarella stick in cornstarch, then dip and coat in the egg, and then coat well in the almond flour mixture. Coat each mozzarella piece well with the batter to enclose the cheese in the mixture so it doesn't spread onto the baking sheet while baking. Place each coated mozzarella piece on a large plate. Repeat until all the mozzarella pieces are coated.

Cover the plate with plastic wrap and place the mozzarella sticks in the freezer for about 2 hours.

Preheat the oven to 400°F. Line a baking sheet with parchment paper.

Place the mozzarella pieces about 1-inch apart on the baking sheet. Using a basting brush, coat each side of each mozzarella piece lightly with the oil.

Bake for 4 to 6 minutes, until the cheese starts to bubble, and the crust starts to turn slightly golden. Watch closely to make sure the cheese does not start to spread. Enjoy warm.

Nutrition (2 MOZZARELLA STICKS): Calories: 182; Protein: 11g; Fat: 15g; Carbohydrates: 4g; Fiber: 1g; Sugar: 1g; Sodium: 311mg

Almond Light-as-Air Cookies

Preparation Time: 5 minutes
Cooking Time: 10 minutes
Servings: 8
Ingredients:
8 tablespoons almond flour
1 tablespoon low-sugar vanilla whey protein powder
1 tablespoon whipped butter
2 teaspoons vanilla extract
1 teaspoon baking powder
1 teaspoon finely granulated pure cane sugar
½ teaspoon stevia or no-calorie sweetener
¼ teaspoon salt
Directions:

Preheat the oven to 350°F. Line a large baking sheet with parchment paper.

In a large bowl, combine the almond flour, protein powder, whipped butter, vanilla extract, baking powder, sugar, stevia, and salt and mix well until fully incorporated.

Scoop heaping tablespoons of the mixture onto the baking sheet about an inch apart. Using a spatula, flatten the batter slightly into about 2-inch circles. This should yield 8 cookies.

Bake for 7 to 9 minutes, or until the edges of cookies are slightly golden brown. Keep a close eye on the cookies since as soon as this happens, you will want to remove the cookies from the oven to prevent overcooking. Allow the cookies to cool slightly before serving.

Nutrition: (2 COOKIES): Calories: 117; Protein: 6g; Fat: 9g; Carbohydrates: 5g; Fiber: 2g; Sugar: 2g; Sodium: 288mg

Strawberry Gelatin Tea

Preparation Time: 5 minutes
Cooking Time: 5 minutes
Servings: 1
Ingredients:
½ cup frozen sliced strawberries
¼ teaspoon stevia or no-calorie sweetener
½ cup hot water
2 tablespoons plain gelatin powder
Directions:

In a small saucepan, cook the strawberries over medium heat for 3 minutes, stirring frequently, until softened.

Stir in the stevia. Remove the pan from the heat and set aside.

Pour the hot water into a mug. Mix in the gelatin powder a bit at a time while continuously stirring with a fork. Keep stirring as you add in the cooked strawberries.

Blend the mixture in a blender for about 30 seconds, until frothy.

Pour into a mug. Sip once cooled and enjoy as a tea within about 15 minutes or so before it starts to set.

Nutrition: (¾ CUP OR 12 TABLESPOONS): Calories: 89; Protein: 12g; Fat: 0g; Carbohydrates: 10g; Fiber: 2g; Sugar: 5g; Sodium: 47mg

• Subtly Sweet Coconut Milk "Flan"

Preparation Time: 5 minutes
Cooking Time: 5 minutes
Servings: 1
Ingredients:
½ cup light unsweetened coconut milk
2 teaspoons vanilla extract
1 teaspoon stevia or no-calorie sweetener
1 tablespoon (1 packet) plain gelatin powder
Directions:

In a small saucepan, heat the coconut milk for 1 to 2 minutes, then sprinkle in the vanilla extract and stevia and stir to dissolve.

Sprinkle in the gelatin while stirring constantly to dissolve the gelatin completely. Remove from the heat.

Transfer the mixture to a blender and blend for about 30 seconds or so, until frothy. Pour into a small jar or mug.

Allow the dessert to set in the refrigerator for about an hour to firm.

Serve and enjoy.

Nutrition: (6 TABLESPOONS): Calories: 130; Protein: 6g; Fat: 7g; Carbohydrates: 5g; Fiber: 0g; Sugar: 3g; Sodium: 51mg

• Chia Chocolate Pudding

Preparation Time: 5 minutes
Cooking Time: 2 hours
Servings: 1
Ingredients:
½ cup unsweetened almond milk
½ cup nonfat plain Greek yogurt
2 tablespoons chia seeds
1 tablespoon vanilla whey protein
1 teaspoon unsweetened cocoa powder
½ teaspoon stevia or no-calorie sweetener
Directions:

In a canning jar, combine the almond milk, yogurt, chia seeds, whey protein, cocoa powder, and stevia. Seal with lid and let sit in refrigerator overnight. Enjoy straight from the jar, or in a separate bowl if you are consuming a smaller serving.

Nutrition: (1¼ CUP): Calories: 257; Protein: 25g; Fat: 12g; Carbohydrates: 21g; Fiber: 11g; Sugar: 5g; Sodium: 122mg

Simply Vanilla Frozen Greek Yogurt

Preparation Time: 5 minutes
Cooking Time: 8 hours
Servings: 4
Ingredients:
4 cups nonfat plain Greek yogurt
4 tablespoons vanilla whey protein powder
4 tablespoons vanilla extract
4 teaspoons stevia or no-calorie sweetener
Directions:

In a large bowl or loaf pan, combine the yogurt, protein powder, vanilla extract, and stevia.

Cover and freeze overnight or for at least 8 hours.

About an hour before serving, set in the refrigerator to thaw slightly. Serve and enjoy.

Nutrition: (1 CUP): Calories: 183; Protein: 28g; Fat: 1g; Carbohydrates: 12g; Fiber: 1g; Sugar: 8g; Sodium: 96mg

• Mashed Cauliflower

Preparation Time: 10 MINUTES
Cooking Time: 5 MINUTES
Servings: 4
Ingredients:
1 large head cauliflower
¼ cup water
1/3 cup low-fat buttermilk
1 tablespoon minced garlic
1 tablespoon extra-virgin olive oil

Directions:
Break the cauliflower into small florets. Place in a large microwave-safe bowl with the water. Cover and microwave for about 5 minutes, or until the cauliflower is soft. Drain the water from the bowl.
Using a food processor, puree the buttermilk, cauliflower, garlic, and olive oil on medium speed until the cauliflower is smooth and creamy.
Serve immediately.
Ingredient tip: You can buy buttermilk in most supermarkets, but it's just as easy to make your own. Mix 1 teaspoon freshly squeezed lemon juice with 1/3 cup low-fat milk. Let the mixture sit for about 10 minutes, or until the milk begins to thicken.
Cooking tip: For even more flavor, microwave the cauliflower with chicken or vegetable broth instead of water and add ½ cup shredded Parmigiano-Reggiano cheese when you puree the mixture. You can add protein to this dish by blending in powdered egg whites or unflavored protein powder after the first puree (puree until smooth and creamy; then add the protein powder and puree to incorporate).
Nutrition:
Per Serving (½ cup): Calories: 62; Total fat: 2g; Protein: 3g; Carbs: 8g; Fiber: 3g; Sugar: 3g; Sodium: 54mg

• Baked Zucchini Fries

Preparation Time: 15 Minutes
Cooking Time: 30 Minutes
Servings: 6
Ingredients
3 large zucchini
2 large eggs
1 cup whole-wheat bread crumbs
¼ cup shredded Parmigiano-Reggiano cheese
1 teaspoon garlic powder
1 teaspoon onion powder
Directions:
Preheat the oven to 425°F
Halve each zucchini lengthwise and continue slicing each piece into fries about ½ inch in diameter. You will have about 8 strips per zucchini.
In a small bowl, crack the eggs and beat lightly.
In a medium bowl, combine the bread crumbs, Parmigiano-Reggiano cheese, garlic powder, and onion powder.
One by one, dip each zucchini strip into the egg, then roll it in the bread crumb mixture. Place on the prepared baking sheet.
Roast for 30 minutes, stirring the fries halfway through. Zucchini fries are done when brown and crispy.
Serve immediately.
NUTRITION:
Per Serving (4 fries): Calories: 89; Total fat: 3g; Protein: 5g; Carbs: 10g; Fiber: 1g; Sugar: 3g; Sodium: 179mg

• Pickle Roll-Ups

Preparation Time: 20 Minutes
Cooking Time: 20 Minutes
Ingredients
¼ pound deli ham (nitrate-free), thinly sliced (about 8 slices)
8 ounces cheese, at room temperature
1 teaspoon dried dill
1 teaspoon onion powder
8 whole kosher dill pickle spears
Directions:
Get a large cutting board or clean counter space to assemble your roll-ups.
Lay the ham slices on the work surface and carefully spread on the cheese.
Season each lightly with the dill and onion powder.
Place an entire pickle on an end of the ham and carefully roll.

Slice each pickle roll-up into mini rounds about ½- to 1-inch wide.
Skew each with a toothpick for easier serving.
Nutrition:
Per Serving (1 roll-up): Calories: 86; Total fat: 7g; Protein: 4g; Carbs: 4g; Fiber: 0 g; Sugar: 2g; Sodium: 540mg

• Tomato, Basil, And Cucumber Salad

Preparation Time: 15 Minutes
Cooking Time: 30 Minutes
Servings: 6
Ingredients
1 large cucumber, seeded and sliced
4 medium tomatoes, quartered
1 medium red onion, thinly sliced
½ cup chopped fresh basil
3 tablespoons red wine vinegar
1 tablespoon extra-virgin olive oil
½ teaspoon Dijon mustard
½ teaspoon freshly ground black pepper
DIRECTIONS:
In a medium bowl, mix together the cucumber, tomatoes, red onion, and basil.
In a small bowl, whisk together the vinegar, olive oil, mustard, and pepper.
Pour the dressing over the vegetables, and gently stir until well combined.
Cover and chill for at least 30 minutes prior to serving.
NUTRITION:
Per Serving (½ cup): Calories: 72; Total fat: 4g; Protein: 1g; Carbs: 8g; Fiber: 1g; Sugar: 4g; Sodium: 5mg

• Raspberry Sorbet

Preparation time: 10 min
Cooking time: 0 min
Servings: 2
Ingredients:
Honey (1 Tbsp.)
Coconut water (.25 c.)
Raspberries (12 oz.)
Directions:
We need to take all of those ingredients that we listed above and add them inside a prepared blender. Blend until it is nice and smooth. Pour this into a container and add the lid to the top. Add to the freezer to set for a few hours before serving.
Nutrition: Calories 131, Fat 4, Carbs 8, Protein 6, Sodium 212

• Avocado Hummus

Preparation time: 15 min
Cooking time: 0 min
Servings: 2
Ingredients:
Edamame (1 c.)
Chopped avocado (.5)
Lemon juice (1 Tbsp.)
Olive oil (2 Tbsp.)
Minced garlic (.5 tsp.)
Onion powder (.5 tsp.)
Tahini (1 tsp.)
Directions: Add all of these ingredients into a blender and blend to make smooth. Serve with some vegetables and enjoy it.
Nutrition: Calories 112, Fat 4, Carbs 18, Protein 7, Sodium 126

Avocado Detox Smoothie

Preparation time: 10 minutes
Cooking time: - 30 minutes
Sevings: 2
Ingredients:
½ avocado, peeled and roughly chopped
1 banana, peeled and chopped
Handful baby spinach, torn
1 tbsp powdered stevia
1 tsp turmeric, ground
1 tbsp flaxseed, ground
1 tbsp goji berries
Directions:
Peel the avocado and cut in half. Remove the pit and chop one half into small pieces. Wrap the other half in a plastic foil and refrigerate for later.
Peel the banana and cut into thin slices. Set aside.
Rinse the spinach thoroughly under cold running water using a colander. Chop into small pieces and set aside.
Now, combine avocado, banana, spinach, turmeric, flaxseed, and goji berries in a blender. Process until well combined.
Transfer to a serving glass and add few ice cubes. Serve immediately.
Nutrition information per serving: Calories: 221, Protein: 3.1g, Total Carbs: 28.6g, Dietary Fibers: 7.5g, Total Fat: 11.8g

Sweet Pumpkin Pudding

Preparation time: 15 minutes
Cooking time: 15 minutes
Servings: 4
Ingredients:
1 lb pumpkin, peeled and chopped into bite-sized pieces
2 tbsp honey
½ cup cornstarch
4 cups pumpkin juice, unsweetened
1 tsp cinnamon, ground
3 cloves, freshly ground
Directions:
Peel and prepare the pumpkin. Scrape out seeds and chop into bite-sized pieces. Set aside.
In a small bowl, combine pumpkin juice, honey, orange juice, cinnamon, and cornstarch.
Place the pumpkin chops in a large pot and pour the pumpkin juice mixture. Stir well and then finally add cloves. Stir until well incorporated and heat up until almost boiling. Reduce the heat to low and cook for about 15 minutes, or until the mixture thickens.
Remove from the heat and transfer to the bowls immediately. Set aside to cool completely and then refrigerate for 15 minutes before serving, or simply chill overnight.
Nutrition information per serving: Calories: 232, Protein: 2.7g, Total Carbs: 56g, Dietary Fibers: 4.6g, Total Fat: 0.9g

Beet Spinach Salad

Preparation time:15-20 minutes
Cooking time: 40 minutes
Servings: 3
Ingredients:
2 medium-sized beet, trimmed and sliced
1 cup fresh spinach, chopped
2 spring onions, finely chopped
1 small green apple, cored and chopped
3 tbsp olive oil
2 tbsp fresh lime juice
1 tbsp honey, raw
1 tsp apple cider vinegar
1 tsp salt
Directions:
Wash the beets and trim off the green parts. Set aside.
Wash the spinach thoroughly and drain. Cut into small pieces and set aside.
Wash the apple and cut lengthwise in half. Remove the core and cut into bite-sized pieces and set aside.
Wash the onions and cut into small pieces. Set aside.
In a small bowl, combine olive oil, lime juice, honey, vinegar, and salt. Stir until well incorporated and set aside to allow flavors to meld.
Place the beets in a deep pot. Pour enough water to cover and cook for about 40 minutes, or until tender. Remove the skin and slice. Set aside.
In a large salad bowl, combine beets, spinach, spring onions, and apple. Stir well until combined and drizzle

with previously prepared dressing. Give it a good final stir and serve immediately.
Nutrition information per serving: Calories: 215, Protein: 1.8g, Total Carbs: 23.8g, Dietary Fibers: 3.6g, Total Fat: 14.3g

• Grilled Avocado in Curry Sauce

Preparation time: 15 minutes
Cooking time: 25-30 minutes
Servings: 2
Ingredients:
1 large avocado, chopped
¼ cup water
1 tbsp curry, ground
2 tbsp olive oil
1 tsp soy sauce
1 tsp fresh parsley, finely chopped
¼ tsp red pepper flakes
¼ tsp sea salt
Directions:
Peel the avocado and cut lengthwise in half. Remove the pit and cut the remaining avocado into small chunks. Set aside.
Heat up the olive oil in a large saucepan over a medium-high temperature.
In a small bowl, combine ground curry, soy sauce, parsley, red pepper and sea salt. Add water and cook for about 5 minutes, stirring occasionally.
Add chopped avocado, stir well and cook for 3 more minutes, or until all the liquid evaporates. Turn off the heat and cover. Let it stand for about 15-20 minutes before serving.
Nutrition information per serving: Calories: 338, Protein: 2.5g, Total Carbs: 10.8g, Dietary Fibers: 7.9g, Total Fat: 34.1g

Broccoli Cauliflower Puree

Preparation time: 10-15 minutes
Cooking time: 15-20 minutes
Servings: 2
Ingredients:
2 cups fresh broccoli chopped
2 cups fresh cauliflower, chopped
½ cup skim milk
½ tsp salt
½ tsp Italian seasoning
¼ tsp cumin, ground
1 tbsp fresh parsley, finely chopped
1 tbsp olive oil
1 tsp dry mint, ground
Directions:
Wash and roughly chop the cauliflower. Place it in a deep pot and add a pinch of salt. Cook for about 15-20 minutes. When done, drain and transfer it to a food processor. Set aside.
Wash the broccoli and chop into bite-sized pieces. Add it to the food processor along with milk, salt, Italian seasoning, cumin, parsley, and mint. Gradually add olive oil and blend until nicely pureed.
Serve with some fresh carrots and celery.
Nutrition information per serving: Calories: 138, Protein: 6.1g, Total Carbs: 12.7g, Dietary Fibers: 4.6g, Total Fat: 7.5g

• Peanut butter joy cookies

Preparation time: 30 min
Cooking time: 45 min
Servings: 3-4
Ingredients:
250 ml quick oats
250 ml peanut butter, unsweetened
250 ml Splenda 1 tsp vanilla
1/2 tsp cinnamon, dried 1 egg
Directions:
Pre-heat oven to 350 degrees.
Place the peanut butter and Splenda in a mixing bowl. Using a sturdy spoon or hand beaters, beat the two together until smooth. Add in the egg, keep mixing, then add the vanilla.
Last, add in the oats and cinnamon. Continue to mix until everything is nice smooth dough.
Scoop the dough out a by dessert spoon and using your hands, roll into balls. Place the balls on a cookie sheet and squish them gently down with a fork.
Place cookies in the oven for eight min until golden brown. Wait for them to cool before lifting off the pan.
Nutrition information per serving: Calories: 338, Protein: 2.5g, Total Carbs: 10.8g, Dietary Fibers: 7.9g, Total Fat: 34.1g

Chocolate almond ginger mousse

Preparation time: 10 min
Cooking time: 30 min (4 hours cooling time)
Servings: 5
Ingredients:
325 ml milk, skim & cold
1 instant pudding package, fat-free and sugar-free
250 ml cool whip lite, thawed out
1/4 tsp ginger, dried
1 tbsp almonds, sliced
Directions:
Pour cold milk into a mixing bowl. Beating steadily with wire whisk, add the pudding mix and dried ginger. Keep whisking for two min. Fold in the cool whip topping.
Spoon into five pudding cups, refrigerate until needed. Garnish with sliced almonds just before servings.
Nutrition: Servings: 1g calories: 310kcal carbohydrates: 21g protein: 3.9g fat: 26.4g saturated fat: 9.5g polyunsaturated fat: 16.9g odium: 90mg fiber: 10.2g sugar: 7.1g

Bella's apple crisp

Preparation time: 20 min
Cooking time: 20 min
Servings: 4
Ingredients:
Four apples, hard and crisp, cored and sliced
1/2 lemon
2 tbsp water
2 tbsp agave nectar or one tbsp honey
Ingredients for toppings:
200 ml old-fashioned rolled oats
2 tbsp butter, cold
1/2 tsp cinnamon
125 ml chopped walnuts
Directions:
Heat oven to 350 degrees.
Place sliced apples in the bottom of an eight-inch pie plate or square cake pan.
Drizzle the water, lemon juice, and syrup over the apples.
In a mixing bowl, stir together the oats and cinnamon. Use a pastry cutter or two knives to cut in the butter mixture until it resembles coarse breadcrumbs.
Stir in the chopped nuts.
Sprinkle the mixture over the apples covering them completely.
Cover pan with tin foil and slide into the middle of the oven for twenty min.
Remove tin foil from pan and continue to bake for another ten to fifteen min until topping is golden brown.
Option: Servings: with a dab of fat-free, sugar-free ice cream.
Nutrition:
Calories: 424kcal carbohydrates: 74.3g
protein: 14.6g fat: 9.4g
saturated fat: 2g
polyunsaturated fat: 7.4g
cholesterol: 94mg sodium: 572mg
fiber: 11.3g
sugar: 24.2g

Red energy wonders

Preparation time: 15 min
Cooking time: 15 min
Servings: 5-6
Ingredients:
75 ml almond butter
325 ml coconut, shredded and divided into a 225 ml portion and a 100 ml portion
125 ml oats, rolled 125 ml of strawberries
125 ml almonds 4 dates, Medrol, pit-less
Directions:
Place the 225 portions of coconut and all the rest of the ingredients in a food processor. On high speed, process until smooth and fully mixed.
Pour the remaining coconut onto a plate. With a spoon, scoop out one tablespoon of the mixture and form into a ball. Roll this ball around in the coconut, then place on a plate lined with parchment paper. Repeat until all of the mixtures are used.
Place the plate in the fridge for at least two hours before servings. Keep energy wonders in an airtight container in the fridge.
Nutrition:

Calories: 191kcal carbohydrates: 17.9g protein: 6.3g fat: 12g saturated fat: 5.4g polyunsaturated fat: 6.6g cholesterol: 7mg sodium: 101mg fiber: 2.8g sugar: 8.6g

Chocolate protein pudding pops

Preparation time: 5 min,
Cooking Time: 10 minutes
Servings: 4
Ingredients:
1 (3.9-ounce) package chocolate-flavored instant pudding
2 cups cold low-fat milk
2 scoops chocolate protein powder
Directions:
In a medium bowl, whisk the pudding mix, milk, and protein powder for at least 2 min.
Spoon into ice pop molds or paper cups. Insert an ice pop stick into the center of each mold or cup.
Freeze for 4 hours, or until firm. Remove from the molds or cups before servings.
Post-op Servings: suggestions
Nutrition:
Nutrition: calories: 215; total fat: 2g; protein: 12g; carbohydrates: 36g; fiber: 0g; sugar: 27g; sodium: 480mg.

Strawberry frozen yogurt

Preparation time: 5 min
Cooking Time: 4 hours
Servings: 4
Ingredients:
2 tablespoons honey
1 cup low-fat, plain Greek yogurt
4 cups frozen strawberries
2 teaspoons vanilla extract
1 teaspoon freshly squeezed lemon juice
Directions:
In a food processor combine the yogurt, strawberries, honey, vanilla, and lemon juice. Pulse until crumbly, then process until the mixture becomes creamy. Transfer to a standard-size loaf pan. Cover and freeze for 2 hours, or until frozen but still soft enough to scoop, and servings. Post-op Servings: suggestions Ingredient tip: berries are a great source of fiber and antioxidants and a wonderful addition to your diet. Switch it up and try this recipe with raspberries, blueberries, cranberries, or whatever you find in season and available.
Nutrition:
Nutrition: calories: 135; total fat: 1g; protein: 6g; carbohydrates: 25g; fiber: 3g; sugar: 17g; sodium: 39mg.

Lemon mousse

Preparation time: 15 min,
Cooking Time: 4 hours 15 min
Servings: 4
Ingredients:
1½ cups boiling water
1 (6-ounce) package sugar-free lemon-flavored gelatin
2 cups ice cubes 1½ cups whipped topping
Fresh fruit, for Servings: (optional)
Directions:
In a large bowl, combine the boiling water and gelatin. Stir for at least 2 min, or until the gelatin is completely dissolved. Add the ice cubes, and stir until melted. Refrigerate until thickened, 5 to 10 min.
Fold in the whipped topping. Divide into four portions and refrigerate until firm, about 4 hours.
Garnish with fresh fruit before Servings: (if desired).
Post-op Servings: suggestions
Nutrition:
Nutrition: calories: 85; total fat: 6g; protein: 1g; carbohydrates: 6g; fiber: 0g; sugar: 3g; sodium: 45mg.

Mozzarella Balls Recipe

Preparation Time: 10 minutes
Cooking Time: 5 minutes
Servings: 8 servings
Ingredients
1 package string cheese
2 cups of Panko Bread Crumbs
2 tsp Italian seasoning
1 tsp parsley
1 cup of milk
1 cup of flour
Marinara Sauce (homemade or store bought)
Oil for frying
Direction:
Split 1-inch pieces of string cheese
In a bowl By pouring milk and setting aside, prepare the coating form. Put 1 cup of flour in a plastic bag and add 2 cups of panko, mixed with seasonings, into another bag.
Place the cheese, one handful at a time, in the milk.
Toss it in your bag of flour and shake well.
Put the cheese back in your bowl of milk, then coat it full.
Toss and shake in the panko bag until uniformly covered.
Place bites of mozzarella on a plate or in a bag and freeze for a minimum of 2 hours.
Heat oil on medium heat. Fry until golden brown in hot oil. Be sure to take out them of the oil until they get too hot, or from the breading, cheese will ooze.
With marinara sauce, serve soft. ENJOY!
Nutrition:
Amount Per Serving
Fat 1g; Cholesterol 3mg; Sodium 124mg; Potassium 92mg; Carbohydrates 24g; Fiber 1g; Sugar 2g; Protein 4g; Vitamin A 55IU; Calcium 71mg; Iron 1.6mg

Chocolate Protein Balls

Preparation time: 40 mins
Cooking time: 0 mins
Servings: 10
Ingredients
1 cup of rolled oats
½ cup of natural peanut butter
⅓ cup of honey
¼ cup of chopped dark chocolate
2 tbsp flax seeds
2 tbsp chia seeds
1 tbsp chocolate-flavored protein powder, or as need
Directions
In a bowl, whisk together the oats, peanut butter, honey, chocolate, flax seeds, chia seeds and protein powder until mixed evenly. Cover the plastic wrap with a bowl and refrigerate for 30 minutes.
Scoop the balls into a chilled mixture. Keep it cold before you serve.
Nutrition Per Serving:
188 calories; protein 5.8g 12% DV; carbohydrates 21.5g 7% DV; fat 9.9g 15% DV; cholesterol 0.2mg; sodium 67.5mg 3% DV.

Instant Frozen Berry Yogurt

Preparation time: 2 mins
Cooking time: 0 minutes
Serving: 4
Ingredients
250g frozen mixed berry
250g Greek yogurt
1 tbsp honey
Direction:
In a food processor, mix the berries, yogurt, and honey or agave syrup for 20 seconds, until the ice cream texture is smooth. Scoop and serve in bowls.
Nutrition: per serving
low in kcal 70; fat 0g; carbs 10g; sugars 10g; fiber 2g; protein 7g; low in salt 0.1g

Chocolate Avocado Pudding

Preparation time: 40 mins
Cooking time: 0 mins
Servings: 4
Ingredients
2 large avocados - peeled, pitted, and cubed
½ cup of unsweetened cocoa powder
½ cup of brown sugar
⅓ cup of coconut milk
2 tsp vanilla extract

1 pinch ground cinnamon

Directions

In a blender, mix the avocado, cocoa powder, brown sugar, coconut milk, vanilla extract, and cinnamon until soft. Refrigerate the pudding for about 30 minutes until it is chilled

Nutrition Per Serving:

400 calories; protein 5.4g 11% DV; carbohydrates 45.9g 15% DV; fat 26.3g 41% DV; sodium 22.6mg 1% DV.

• Mixed Berry Popsicles

Preparation Time: 1 Hr
Cooking Time: 4 Hrs
Servings: 10 Popsicles

Ingredients

1 cup of blackberries
1 cup of boysenberries
1 cup of strawberries
1 cup of raspberries
4 tbsp honey
4 tsp lemon juice

Direction:

In your food processor, put the blackberries. Add 1 tbsp of honey and 1 tsp of lemon juice. Pulse until a fine puree is available to you.

In your popsicle molds, pour the blackberry puree into the rim. Place it for 15 minutes in the freezer.

When your popsicle mold is in the fridge, wash your food processor.

Boysenberries, then raspberries and eventually strawberries repeat the first two stages.

In your popsicle mold, put your popsicle sticks and place them in the freezer for at least 4 hours to harden fully.

Nutrition

CALORIES: 49kcal, CARBOHYDRATES: 12g, POTASSIUM: 86mg, FIBER: 2g, SUGAR: 9g, VITAMIN A: 40iu, VITAMIN C: 15.8mg, CALCIUM: 13mg, IRON: 0.4mg

Conclusion

Choosing to switch to a weight-loss plan can be difficult. But, if you have chosen the gastric sleeve surgery, then it's essential that you know how to eat after this surgery. Eating the right foods will help you on your way not only in losing weight but also in feeling better. This cookbook is for anyone who has undergone gastric sleeve bariatric surgery and wants to enjoy food while losing weight; without medication, diet pills, or any other type of drugs. In this cookbook are over 100 delicious recipes that are surprisingly easy and quick enough for a busy lifestyle.

Thousands of people are going through this difficult surgery and many of them come out with no weight loss. By knowing how to eat after gastric sleeve surgery, you will be able to eat in a healthier way and still lose weight. You'll save money, and I promise you that you'll have more energy, better moods, and feel better overall.

This is a book that can help you lose weight by eating the right foods in a healthy way. So if you are thinking about this surgery or have already had it done, please read this cookbook now.

If you are thinking about gastric sleeve bariatric surgery, then this is the cookbook you need. It's full of delicious recipes that are healthy, low in calories and low in carbohydrates. Get no more than 50 grams of carbohydrates per day, because you must stay lean. If you don't stay lean, then it's not a good idea to lose weight. This cookbook will help you lose weight but keep your lean body mass up.

"Eating right" for weight loss means consuming few calories and lots of nutrients. You must eat protein in order to keep lean, so be sure to include some meat with every meal. Any excess protein, however, will be converted into carbohydrates in your body.

This cookbook will also help you lose a lot of fat which is the most important step towards weight loss.

Fats are necessary for a healthy diet, but eating too much will slow down your weight loss progress considerably. If you are not losing weight as fast as you'd like, try this cookbook out and see how much fat is cut out of your diet.

Gastric sleeve bariatric surgery is a great way to get your eating habits fixed and your weight loss started in the right direction. It's still up to you, however, if you want to succeed. This cookbook is here to help you fix your eating habits and lose weight effectively.

This cookbook can help those who have had problems with losing weight, like binge eating or emotional eating.

The recipes in this cookbook will help you repair your relationship with food and lose the excess weight that has been bothering you for so long.

You are about to learn how easy it is to eat a healthy diet of lean protein, healthy fats, lots of vegetables and fruits and still lose weight. By switching your eating habits around with the recipes in this cookbook, you will finally begin losing weight and feeling better overall.

With the loss of all that excess fat, you will not only look better but feel better too. Your blood pressure may even lower and you'll be able to eliminate a lot of stress as well as unwanted pounds from your life.

This cookbook is very easy to follow and you can start eating healthy today.

Printed in Great Britain
by Amazon